Eva +
Cam

THE BOOK OF JAMES

Susy Smith

THE BOOK OF JAMES

William James, That Is

toExcel
San Jose New York Lincoln Shanghai

The Book of James (William James, That is)
Conversations From Beyond

All Rights Reserved © 1974, 2000 by Susy Smith

No part of this book may be reproduced or transmitted in any form or by any means, graphic, electronic, or mechanical, including photocopying, recording, taping, or by any information storage or retrieval system, without the permission in writing from the publisher.

Published by toExcel
an imprint of iUniverse.com, Inc.

For information address:
iUniverse.com, Inc.
620 North 48th Street
Suite 201
Lincoln, NE 68504-3467
www.iuniverse.com

ISBN: 1-58348-573-2

Printed in the United States of America

I can conceive of no greater service to man than to provide him with a credible picture of a life beyond death; a life which reunites him with those whom he has loved and have died, which makes sense of his striving and suffering on earth, which points to love as the principle of the universe, and which shows a progression towards ultimate union with that love which is God.

"The Nature of Life after Death"
—ALLAN BARHAM

CONTENTS

1	THE COMING OF JAMES	11
2	JAMES BEGINS AND TALKS ABOUT GOD	20
3	THE UNOBSTRUCTED DIMENSIONS OF LIFE	26
4	THE CLOSED MIND AND WHERE IT GETS YOU	34
5	INFORMATION ABOUT THE HUMAN MIND	42
6	HOW TO USE YOUR THOUGHTS EFFECTIVELY	48
7	THE GRADUAL TRANSITION	57
8	THE PLEASURES OF PARADISE	65
9	STARTING UPWARD	74
10	THE GOLDEN CHAIN	81
11	THE SAD, SAD STATE OF THE EARTHBOUND	90
12	SEX BETWEEN THE SPHERES	96
13	ANGELS AND GODS ARE REAL	101
14	BABIES COME AND BABIES GO	110
15	REINCARNATION	116
16	*THE EXORCIST* REVISITED	126
17	MEDIUMS ARE A NECESSITY	137
18	CHILDREN ARE TO BE CHERISHED	144
19	ANIMALS ARE FOREVER	153
20	SUICIDE IS NOT RECOMMENDED	159
21	OUT-OF-THE-BODY TRAVEL	166
22	QUESTIONS AND ANSWERS	172
23	THE END IS JUST THE BEGINNING	184
	BIBLIOGRAPHY	189

THE BOOK OF JAMES

I

THE COMING OF JAMES

It may surprise you that I, an author of twenty-three books on the research and investigation of psychic subjects, should now offer a volume I did *not* write—at least, I did not write it *consciously*. This book contains so much information new and foreign to me that I am certain it did not come from me. I truly believe, after many years of doubt and critical evaluation, that the spirit of a man who once lived on earth wrote it, using my hands on the typewriter keys as his means of expression.

I have spent nearly twenty years learning to be receptive to the supraphysical world. Throughout this time, during many exciting adventures researching and writing, traveling and lecturing, I have also been developing my psychic abilities and attempting to become a clear channel for spirit communication. This book is the culmination of my efforts.

Naturally I questioned the source of the following material, debating it constantly for many years. Did it really come, as it purports to, from entities now surviving in spiritual dimensions of life? Or have I in some way tapped the universal unconscious? Might it be possible that my own subconscious, with strange unfathomable powers, has gathered together bits of this and that from other writers, added a great deal to them, clarified them, and then poured forth a synthesis of them as automatic writing? There are several facts that confound this theory, the prime one being my prior life-long indifference to philosophy. Even after I became interested in psychical phenomena, I read only "objective" books, not those written by "believers." Yet the material I receive on my typewriter, while providing a great deal of new and revolutionary illumination, confirms astoundingly many other writings I have since consulted—notably those of Emanuel Swedenborg. Oddly enough, it also corresponds in many ways with old-fashioned Spiritualist beliefs, which surprised me very much for I had felt them to be simplistic and naïve. My communicant analyzes, explains and justifies these concepts so well, however, that I now think them definitely worthy of consideration.

I have already told my own history in *Confessions of a Psychic* (Macmillan, 1971), so I will but briefly provide some personal data to prepare you for the coming of James. In college I came to consider myself an agnostic. For many years my philosophy of life was "Always expect the worst and you won't be disappointed." I wasn't disappointed, for the worst came to me in overwhelming measure. I contracted a crippling disease, and numerous operations followed. A short, unhappy marriage ended in divorce. My parents died, and I was left alone in the world. Whenever I thought about it, I thought life was a mess; but I learned to do what most people do: very seldom to ponder religion and philosophy. I simply went on living to the hilt, having as much fun as I could (with my innate sense of gaiety this was possible even in the midst of most problems and perplexities), and thinking less and less about the whys and wherefores.

Finally came the day, in 1955, when I picked up Stewart Edward White's *The Unobstructed Universe* and read his assertion that man survives death in a condition of conscious awareness. He also gave what appeared to be a good bit of proof that he was in actual communication with his deceased wife. "Consciousness is the only reality," he said, "and consciousness is in a state of evolution." Being an evolutionist, I was attracted by this thought. If White's statements were proved scientifically, then existence would make sense to me; so I began an attempt to have genuine supernormal experiences of my own in order to acquire personal evidence.

I soon found in the library the books of Dr. J. B. Rhine, who was then at the Duke University Parapsychology Laboratory. From them I was impressed that there might be a systematic way to research this subject. It was true that at that time no scientific efforts were being made to determine human survival after death, but the work of Dr. Rhine and other psychical researchers inclined in that general direction. There, apparently, was the area in which to start my investigation, so I began reading everything I could lay my hands on about parapsychology.

I was then a free-lance newspaper columnist. I had no dependents except a miniature dachshund named Junior, and I had recently inherited enough money to support the two of us for a year or two. Being able, therefore, to make any changes I wanted to in my living and working habits, I began to devote my life exclusively to seeking evidence either proving or disproving this new, enticing concept.

From then on I was a searcher, feeling myself to be on the track of something big, but unwilling to admit enough evidence existed to convince me fully of its authenticity. I read avidly all the scientific material available to me on psychical phenomena, a subject that always seems to dangle the promise of proof before one like a carrot before a donkey, but that so seldom fulfills its promise. I read little of the philosophical aspects of the subject, because it was *fact* I wanted, not theory.

I was fortunate enough to be allowed to participate in some of the activity at Dr. Rhine's Parapsychology Laboratory during the winter of 1956. There I was trained in critical appraisal and told never to read books that were not objective. I was also warned to evaluate all psychic experiences carefully, for a new researcher is seldom sufficiently detached.

Even though I studied the critical material, historical and current, and employed scientific method, still I made an effort to communicate, just in case some unseen individual wanted to prove to me that he existed. After all, if one is interested in survival research, how else can he find confirmation but by seeking communication with spirits who are endeavoring to verify their existence? But when I used Ouija boards and attempted automatic writing, I encountered many problems and got into much trouble, so I don't recommend that anyone follow my example of trying to contact spirits alone. I know from personal experience that it is nerve-wracking, disconcerting and at times even dangerous.

I kept at it, however, until eventually I sat at my typewriter for many hours every day receiving information about life after death. Since I was learning by then how to protect myself from spirit intruders, and how important it was to judge my communicant by the value of the material he contributed, I felt secure in the work I was doing. It came from my mother at first—and *Confessions of a Psychic* provides in detail the evidence that convinced me of this. Later she introduced me to another invisible individual whom she called James Anderson. She said he knew a great deal more than she did about conditions after death, and he had more power than she to transmit the truth clearly. I asked him about his personal history, and he gave me several facts: He had lived in Massachusetts, had died in 1910 and had fathered children. I did not know it then, but these details apply to the great American psychologist and philosopher William James. I did not then suspect that "Anderson" was a pseudonym; but had he claimed to be a well-known person, I would not have maintained contact with him. I know how easy it is for the wide-eyed to be taken in by fraudulent entities who claim to be noteworthy personages in order to gain an audience.

I communicated for some time with James Anderson, then my typewriter told me I would move to New York. I lived in Florida at the time and had no desire to reside in the big city, and by then my funds were insufficient for an extended stay there. But within two months somehow I found myself established there, and after a few financially rough years, I began to receive grants from the Parapsychology Foundation, which subsidized my writing until I had published several books.

During my time in New York City I visited a number of mediums. Almost every one told me I had a William or a James with me. Finally one sensitive said outright that one of my spirit associates was *the* William James. Later I asked my typewriter who was actually using the name James Anderson and received the reply, "Yes, I really am William James." He pointed out that if he had originally come to me under his true name, I would have rejected him completely, and he was right.

While applying the finishing touches to this material, I was given an unpublished manuscript received some years ago—ostensibly from William James—by the late British medium Maude V. Underhill. Called *The Upward Path*, it is designed to teach people how to live wisely while on earth, so that they will progress more rapidly in spirit planes after death. Many of the statements are of identical purport and even phrased similarly to those provided me for this book. I therefore believe my material comes from the same source, especially since my James accepts the Underhill script as his. He has not acknowledged any of the other published data claiming to come from him, most of which is quite unlike what I receive.

Because William James' name is so often bandied about in the realm of spirit disclosures, one might suspect there is a group over there who use the name as a generic term to cover all their communicating activity. Miss Underhill's writings start: "I, William James, whilom Professor of Psychology and Philosophy at Harvard University, am now the head of a group of progressive schools in the world beyond the veil called death." If this is true, why should it not be possible that many of his pupils, trained specifically in his techniques and as determined as he to spread information about life in future planes of existence (franchised, one might say, to use his name) are the ones who communicate so widely as William James —much like the numerous Fred Astaire dancing schools in which the great Fred has never tapped a toe.

Taking all this into consideration, I do not claim William James himself to be my communicant, and I simply refer to him as James. Here is what he has told me about his identity, however: "I can give no facts which will in any way prove that it is actually William James writing through you, but it is indeed I. Whatever I could offer of a personal nature about my lifetime on earth in an effort to reveal my identity, detractors would counter that the information had been published previously or that some descendant of mine knows the information and so it was acquired by telepathy from the living. When I was on earth, I would have been the first to use this argument. As you know, I was interested in psychical research for most of my life. My father was a Swedenborgian, and our home echoed with discussion of life after death, as described by the great scientist Emanuel Swedenborg after his years of travel in the spirit world. As I grew older and more cynical, I dismissed such talk and approached psychical research entirely from the scientific point of view. Although I saw a good bit of evidence for survival in my study of that excellent medium Leonore Piper, at no time did I conclude anything more definite than, 'I remain uncertain and await more facts.'

"I have acquired more facts now and am happy to impart them to the world. My advanced awareness, as gleaned from Swedenborg's teachings, prepared me for my transition, and my passing was so much easier than that of most of my contemporaries that I very soon came to realize the value of such knowledge. Because I am aware, then, of how important this information can be to one at the moment of death and even for a long time afterward, I am especially eager to offer the facts for public perusal. I am not alone in my efforts. A great many over here are determined to get the truth about survival to you. We know that the lives of all those now on earth will change for the better when they know with certainty that there is no death—that they will endure in a life of continuity."

Certainly William James' graceful writing style is not evident as he communicates through me, but that's my fault, not his. I do occasionally see signs of his famous wit. As far as what he says through me agreeing with what he believed and wrote while on earth, why should it? He now has an entirely new perspective on existence. And he is much more dogmatic in his opinions than he ever was in his writings on earth. He seems to know more *for sure* now than he did then.

But why was I, Susy Smith, the one to receive this information? Mostly because I have been willing to work the long hours required to produce it; but also (and this is the most backhanded compliment I have ever received) because, my communicant implies, I was so dumb. Actually James says it is because I had given up completely on religion and philosophy and had read almost nothing on the subject since my college days, so my mind was like a sieve through which he could strain his thoughts onto the paper in front of me. I am told that one of the big problems of most spirit communication is that it has to fight the preconceived opinions of the recipient.

James maintains that he has been able to transmit through me much of what he wishes the reader to know. Certainly he isn't able to give me any substantial part of the truth he perceives, for my mind accepts only finite terms and, as British psychical researcher Rosalind Heywood says, "How could one convey the idea of water as steam to a person who only knew it as ice?" Our ability to comprehend anything so nebulous—to us—as a spirit sphere of existence is terribly limited. When it is given actual concrete characteristics, it seems so incongruous we hesitate to "buy" it. But James has done the best he can, and I've done the best I can, and he seems relatively satisfied. "However," he advises the reader, "if you do not feel that you can accept the data this book contains, do not worry about it." He doesn't want you to fight against what you read. He says it does not matter whether or not you believe what is presented here. All that matters is that you be exposed to the concept of Evolutionary Soul Progression, as he calls this system. "Then," he says, "when you die, you will remember at least the basic principles, and this will enable you to face your new life armed with truth rather than confused concepts of no value."

The main part of this manuscript was produced in 1967. By February of that year books of mine were ready to come out under the imprints of several good publishers; I was living in a small, easy-to-care-for apartment in Miami's salubrious climate, with a swimming pool outside my front door for exercise and relaxation; and I was not unduly pressured either for time or money. I was sitting regularly once a week with a circle of friends for psychic development but was not aware that my talents had improved to any great extent. In fact I had no idea what my capabilities were; I had been unable to try communication for several years, while traveling around the country researching haunted houses and mediums.

On Wednesday, February 22, 1967, I had dinner at the home of a friend, and afterward we sat in meditation. Suddenly we both began to have an unusually elated feeling, as if something wonderful were about to happen. I almost burst from my skin with the joy that seized me.

Then a voice beyond my control began to speak through my lips. It did not identify itself, but after a brief inspirational dissertation it made the statement: "You are now ready to begin receiving a book by automatic writing, and if you will sit at your typewriter at nine o'clock tomorrow morning the communication will start."

When my own voice returned to me, I promised to keep the date, and I did. I spent almost all of the next seven days at my typewriter and in that one week the entire James book was written through me. I have as witnesses the friends who eagerly gathered evenings to hear me read each day's fresh material. Since I take a week or sometimes considerably longer to write one chapter on my own, the speed with which this came was extraordinary, to say the least.

Since then, from time to time, my communicant and I have edited the material and added to it. The way our editing is done is interesting, and to me evidential in itself. As we are typing, the machine may stop in the midst of a sentence; I wait for a few seconds, wondering what is wrong. Then I say, "Did we make an error?" If I get the mental impression that the answer is yes, I push the typewriter carriage back to the beginning of the sentence or paragraph. Then I use the space bar and move along word by word until the typewriter stops again. I XXXX out that word and let James write in his correction, then we continue with the forward flow.

Of course, I would never presume to change his text without his permission, but if anything is not quite clear to me or is too wordy or difficult to understand, I tell him and he rewords it—unless, as he sometimes does, he remains adamant that he has written exactly what he wants. Often he is willing to accept my suggestion that he should elucidate some obscure point more fully. Sometimes I ask questions his statements raise in my mind and he provides new information in order to clarify things for me . . . or my friends, who have also queried him on occasion.

Some people think that any entity who communicates from the spirit world is omniscient, and that all his sacred words must be left intact. Because of the difficulties of getting immortal thoughts through mortal minds, however, even the very best mediums may color the material unwittingly. Anyone who receives should be wary of this at all times.

James indicates by his way of writing just how human he is. This is actually his aim. He wants us to be aware that he is still a man, now invisible, who has information to impart about little-known and little-understood aspects of the universe. Some have wondered why, if he died in 1910, he can now talk intelligibly about television, split atoms, and jet airplanes. He sometimes even uses our modern expressions, having taken readily to the term "programmed," for instance. This is because his interests are earth's interests and he has seen from his special vantage point everything that happens here. This confirms his statements about how close he and his companions actually are to our plane of existence as long as they desire to remain near to help us.

Early in 1956, my first year of attempted typewritten reception, my hands would be lifted from the keys before we started to write, and held for a moment in the position of prayer. At that time I did not believe there was a god who pays personal attention to those who approach him through prayer, so the significance of that sign escaped me. I eventually decided it was an identifying signature of my communicant.

Now, after receiving James' philosophy all these years and having become deeply religious in my own personal way, when my hands are lifted from the typewriter keys in that position, I understand that I must pray. It's as simple as that. I must pray for help with the work, and for protection. I also know I must surround myself with protective thoughts, and I state firmly, as I have been instructed, that nothing that does not come from God in love and peace may in any way approach me or influence me.

I also insist that contact be established only with wise communicants who will give me the truth. The sincere desire to transmit only *facts* about conditions after death has been very strong in me as the writing has flowed through my fingers.

In conclusion I must say once again that I do not know where this information has come from; but it certainly didn't originate with me. My mind couldn't possibly have produced all this. I hope it came from the surviving spirit who says he dictated it, but whoever it was has my gratitude.

This philosophy stimulates and challenges me. I hope it will stir you, too. As James says, "If we can impress people with the fact that they do survive death, and that the way they live on earth is vitally important because they will survive, then we have done the world an immense favor."

It can't hurt, and it might help to give James' recommendations our deepest consideration . . . just in case.

The following chapters were written by James. My remarks appear in the form of a commentary.

II

JAMES BEGINS AND TALKS ABOUT GOD

THE EXPERIENCE CALLED death is not an ending but a beginning. It is an opening of doors into new and exciting dimensions of existence. You do survive death; and, in an unbelievably exalted state, you will live forever. You survive as *you*, yourself, the person you are now; and you always retain that same individuality, even when you have advanced to the heights of self-improvement.

At death you leave your physical body behind, as if you had slipped out of a coat; but you continue to exist in a form which is just as real to you as the body you wore on earth. Inside your physical body there has always been, from your first inception, a spiritual duplicate, and it is this which survives, accompanied by your Consciousness (or Soul or Spirit). Since it was, from the beginning, the pattern around which the physical body grew, the spirit body is the real you as far as appearance and condition are concerned; and so when you find yourself out of the physical and in this body, you may not be aware at first that any change has occurred. This is especially true because you are usually still in the same general locality you were at the moment before death.

The thing that seems to be most surprising to most people is to learn that there is no abrupt change of personality or place immediately after death. The area in which one finds himself after he has left the physical body—to which we will refer herein as either the Etheric or the Astral plane because those are the terms commonly used when you people write about them—is, in its lower reaches, identical with the earth plane of existence. One leaves this only as he becomes enlightened as to his true state and learns how to progress to more exalted spheres. There are many spheres or planes or levels of attainment, each an advancement over the others. Eventually everyone achieves a state of what we will refer to as angelhood and then godhood. The culmination of all striving is reached only after a long, long time, but it is indeed worth any amount of effort, for it is the state of Ultimate Perfection in which one remains forever in ecstasy.

When a person goes through the experience called death, his relatives and friends who have preceded him are usually there to greet him if there has been warmth between them. They give him such information as they have acquired, and it varies depending upon the condition each was in when he died and whether or not he has learned anything new since. If these entities were low in development, they may not have become aware of much that is new since their passing. If their lives were rich with spiritual significance, they undoubtedly have already learned a great deal and are knowledgeable about their situation and their hopes for the future.

What the wise spirit will tell you is that life is an unending process and that the life force that is in you came to you from the Godhead and will always continue to exist. It acquired conscious identity when you were born on earth and will continue ever afterward to retain this conscious awareness of itself. Life on earth is so designed as to allow you to achieve identification as a distinct individual. Swedenborg said, "Every man is an original creation" and this is true. You will maintain your identity as you continue after death to progress constantly toward becoming totally aware of your unity with the Overall Guiding Principle of the Universe. And you will still have this awareness of self even after you have reached the highest state. Your spiritual growth during your lifetime and after your death is at your own rate of speed, and you must improve all your capabilities and talents to their highest degree before you can leave the lower spheres; but, you will be told, eventually you will become a perfected soul living a life of eternal jubilance and service.

Those of you who are aware at the time of your passing that you will survive death will probably listen when you are given this information, and almost at once you will set your feet on the upward path. Then you will feel a joyous surge of vitality, a buoyance and vibrance that you will never again lose. Do you remember that inner glow of happiness and well-being you have when you are first in love with someone who returns your affection? Spiritual awareness is very much like that, and it continues forever once you have acquired it.

It is your conscious effort to improve yourself, however, that makes your forward progress, and until you are aware of your need to accomplish this you will be unable to advance. Some will not heed this advice for a long time; nevertheless, the height of achievement inevitably comes for all persons. There is no soul who ever remains behind indefinitely. The ultimate destiny for all is to return to a state of constant blissful awareness of unity with God.

The initial thing that must be understood about the Deity is that this is never a man-God, nor a manlike God. In fact because of the many incorrect anthropomorphic and mythological implications surrounding the word "God," I will use it seldom from now on when I speak of the Source of All Power and Intelligence in the universe. I will instead use such terms as Ultimate Perfection, Supreme Intelligence, or Divine Consciousness.

No individual living on earth or progressing in spirit knows enough about Ultimate Perfection to describe it adequately; yet there are certain attributes that I may attempt to impart. It is a state, first of all, of such omnipotence, such magnificence, such magnitude, that it is impossible for us to conceive its immensity and its greatness. Do not at any time confuse the Supreme Intelligence of the universe with man, for man is only one of its many manifestations. It is all-powerful, all-knowing, all-seeing—all of everything. In trying for descriptive phrases that might be used, we could say that Ultimate Perfection is the State of Highest Awareness, Power Most Superlative, Illimitable Love, Infinite Consciousness. Above all it is Intelligence—inconceivable, incredible, incomprehensible intelligence. Nothing that we can in any way imagine can limit its perfection. Everything in the universe has its origin in it and of it. Man, himself, is an integral part of Divine Consciousness, always has been, is now, and always will be.

Man lives his life on earth for one reason, and one reason only —to individualize himself and establish his identity and character. Creation continues eternally from the highest levels, entirely in accord with system and order. The Soul or consciousness of each baby born on the various inhabited planets of the universe comes from Divine Consciousness. Starting from life's experiences on earth and continuing in spirit planes after the transition of death, each individual is in a process of evolution, and he must eventually improve himself to the point of sublimity. He is created for one purpose—to return in a perfected state to augment the nucleus of Supreme Power. In other words, the expanding universe is controlled by an expanding God Consciousness, which is increased by the constant addition of perfected human consciousnesses.

COMMENTARY:
In the script received by Miss Underhill from James it is expressed this way: "Each individual soul can be likened to a unit, a cell in the Mind of God, which must ultimately become aware of all the Living Truth. It is the glorious task of that unit to enter into the whole awareness, once it has become fully conscious of its being and its purpose in relation to the Whole. . . .

"Imagine the Pattern of God, and yourself as a thread in that pattern. That thread is spun of the substance you gather from life's experience. Why not use your imagination to make it beautiful, real, strong, and worthy of being incorporated into the Great Design? It must ultimately be woven into the very fabric of your oversoul; binding your life into the perfect whole which is in accordance with Reality.

"As you see the living pattern, you will say, 'This is what life should mean. Am I carrying out the purpose for which I was created? Can I spin a beautiful thread and weave it into the design, or is my thread twisted and knotted and lustreless? As you arouse this wondering in your mind, you will realize the wisdom of right-thinking, right-imagining."

If you could always maintain your awareness of the fact of your complete oneness with God, your lives would be glorious even before you come over here. But very few are saintly enough to accomplish this. Although perfection is the ideal, you can only attain a relative degree of perfection on the earth plane.

When one is ready to attempt to reach the heights, he is able to understand and appreciate what his place, his powers, his abilities, and his uses will be after he has perfected himself. Then the idea of eternal life as a functioning individual component of Divine Consciousness is not so appalling as it may seem to you now. It is totally inspiring and challenging . . . and acceptable.

Supreme Intelligence has no physical aspects of any kind, except insofar as it is the basic Cause of the existence of all manifestations in the universe—physical, mental and spiritual. Matter is originated by Divine Consciousness; but Divine Consciousness is vastly more than matter, and matter is only one characteristic of it. Matter is a precipitate of energy or force in a form in which it can be used by all aspects of the Divine, including Men. All the planets, stars, and galaxies of the universe exist only for one purpose: their usefulness to the Divine Plan as it is exemplified in human form on all inhabited planets, either by providing places of habitation or as modifiers of the conditions on other planets in order that these others will be habitable. For the human residents of all planets which are inhabited, I will use the term Man as a generic identification. These Men may differ in their physical bodies according to the conditions on the planets on which they exist; but the same type of consciousness that is in earth's men is in the denizens of all other worlds. Some, of course, are much more highly advanced than you are, and some are less so. The physical body, no matter what form it takes, disintegrates at its death and is of no more use. The consciousness of each Man survives the body at death.

The entire universe follows systems and laws that are the same as the natural laws which apply in your world. (And about many of which you are still woefully ignorant.) Nothing in nature occurs by chance. Nothing happens by accident or in a haphazard manner, even though it may seem to do so. I do not mean that every event is predestined, either. It occurs because of the operation of natural laws, including the law of cause and effect. These laws are always in operation and do not change. System always prevails. Even those things that seem to be chance happenings are definitely the result of some cause, although on many occasions you are unaware of what the cause is. When you learn more about the law of cause and effect, you will understand that each event that occurs has a definite reason. Each action, a specific reaction. The great instigating power of Ultimate Perfection conceived the laws and set everything in the universe in operation in accordance with them. Order is constantly maintained. Patterns are invariably conformed to.

Each man is a separate entity with conscious existence apart from every other man, and he will remain so. He will eventually progress to such heights of greatness that he achieves unity with all other men in the state of Divine Consciousness; but this is unity in the way that members of an orchestra perform in unity, or a choir sings in unity. Souls never merge their identity into one another or into the whole. Each spirit is always a unit that knows itself to be one and individual, yet at the same time it is a functioning, self-operating, cooperating, working unit in the overall Divinity.

The pattern for man's existence, then, is this: A Soul or Conscious Awareness of Self becomes manifest at the birth of every baby born on every inhabited planet. It goes through its life cycle learning what it can from the experiences it encounters, dies to the physical body and emerges as a spirit in whatever stage of personal character development it has attained up to that time. No matter how poor a start this entity has, it will someday learn how to uplift itself and begin its joyful advancement. Eventually by its own efforts at self-improvement, and with the help of progressed spirits, angels and gods, it will achieve a state of wisdom and love so superlative that it enriches and increases the universe with its peace and perfection.

III

THE UNOBSTRUCTED DIMENSIONS OF LIFE

THE FIRST PHASE of existence after the experience called death has been adequately described as "unobstructed" in comparison with the earth plane, which is obstructed by matter. To the senses of those of you on earth, matter is solid. To spirits matter is not solid. It is no obstruction to us, for we can pass right through it. Even time as you know it is not an impediment because we are in no way dependent upon time—there is no night or day for us. Distance is no hindrance to us either, for we think ourselves where we wish to be and we are there.

Yet at first we are exactly the same place that you are—in the earth plane, even though we are in a different dimension of it. We are not floating about up in the clouds somewhere; we are just where we always have been, and many of us continue doing the things we always have done. Usually our biggest worry for a while is that you people no longer see us, hear us, or feel our presence. We are now so unobstructed that we no longer exist for you except in your memories. Your senses are designed to keep you in touch with conditions in your realm—but not with ours. We have passed out of the world of matter into the world of spirit, and we have to learn to live with it.

If you were a person of loving kindness, at your death you will very soon find yourself soaring into higher aspects of the Astral plane; and after you have begun your progression, you will gradually withdraw farther and farther away from your close association with your earth existence. Eventually, after you have graduated from the Astral and reached higher planes, you may live anywhere in the universe that you wish to be or where you find yourself useful. But until you become aware of your need to advance, you may remain in your old haunts for a long, long time.

Your thoughts always modify your conditions. If you are unworthy because of having lived wickedly, your surroundings after death are abominably dismal. You move around very little, thinking yourself always to be in a dark fog or gray gloom. When you become aware of the inevitability of progress, conditions for you clear up at once. And after your spiritual rebirth, when you are advancing to the higher aspects of the Astral, your surroundings are increasingly beautiful because your ability to envision and appreciate beauty is improving. The dimensions of life beyond the Etheric, or Astral (remember, I said I would use these terms interchangeably as the name of the next dimension after death), are even more wonderful. I have not seen them, but am told it is almost impossible to imagine their magnificence. Appreciation of them comes entirely from your own expansion of your awareness to where you can encompass such grandeur.

COMMENTARY: *Yogi Ramacharaka says in* The Life Beyond Death: *"There is no scenery on the Astral plane except that furnished by the thought-forms of the souls inhabiting it. Each soul carries his own set of scenery with it, in his imaginative faculties of mind. It follows, of course, that many souls of the same general ideals and tastes inhabiting the same sub-plane, will carry the same mental scenery with them. And, as the power of thought-transference is manifested strongly on the Astral plane, each soul affects the general scenery of the others. In fact, the scenery of each sub-plane, or division thereof, represents the composite ideals and mental images of those inhabiting it. In earth-life, environment largely makes the man—on the Astral plane, man makes his own environment, in accordance with the absolute and unvarying laws of Nature."*

To say that at first spirits continue to live near your planet does not mean that we are in any crowded state. It would be naive to insist that all the billions who have died still cling to their earthly habits and remain near the places where they lived. Most of those who have begun their progression have already experienced a separation from their former world, not only mentally but spatially. Many areas of the universe are filled with life. Although it is life that is invisible to you, it is not long invisible to those who have left their physical bodies behind and started their regeneration. As each individual advances he withdraws more and more from his close connections with his planet and goes outward and away from that world's atmosphere. His progress is physical as well as mental in that distances are involved, and yet to him distance means nothing. He is as close or as far away as he thinks he is.

COMMENTARY:

This was all that was given about this in 1967. Recently I pressed James for more information about where one is after death. I was trying to understand whether actual dimension is involved. He replied:

"I would have to redefine space for you. What you see from your window is distance extending a limited number of miles. I see distance extending to infinity, and that is altogether different. When distance extends to infinity, it returns on itself and goes nowhere at all. So when I tell you that spirits may be in a far area of the universe from earth, I mean it; and yet at the same time if they wished to be on earth, they would be there immediately. It is all in one piece. It is here and there at the same time. It is everywhere, and it is one specific spot. It is all and it is any degree of allness."

That sounded very erudite to me, but I didn't really comprehend it. Before I could say so, however, James wrote: "This is beyond you. Einstein could understand it, or possibly one who has had a deep illumination, but not one with your limited training. I cannot explain it any better, and that is why I have not gone into it before. If you insist on my telling you exactly where a spirit is after death, I can only refer you to the above paragraph. There is no specific spot; from the time he leaves his earth home he is in time rather than in space. And yet he is close to the earth in the early phases of his life in the spirit world, and he is at a distance from it as he progresses."

Each soul travels by thought, and thought alone. If he thinks of someone and wishes to be with him, he is. If he recalls a friend on earth and wants to visit him, he is there immediately. Until your death it will never be possible for you completely to understand the power of thought as it is expressed on other planes of existence; but all activity is thought power. All motion, all effort, all movement of any kind is by thought. No one is able to do anything except as he conceives it mentally, because mind controls everything in the spirit world. And yet thought is so powerful that a reproduction of any strongly visualized object can be constructed of the degrees of energy that exist here. When we have built or originated this object with our thoughts, it actually exists and may be handled, operated, and used just as you would use a similar object that is palpable to your physical senses. The matter you know on earth is a very much slowed-down form of energy.

If you have advanced spiritually to the point where you do not concentrate much on the earthly conditions with which you once were so familiar, you are not then as closely involved with them, and your presence is withdrawn from them. When you concentrate on any person or event on earth, you are immediately present at that locale and able to participate in what is happening; although, of course, you are invisible to mortals and they are not likely to be aware of your presence.

Time is just as ephemeral here; and yet also just as real. It exists if we think of it and become involved with it; but unless we do, time does not affect us. Our sense of time is different from yours; yet you know that time also varies on your planet. When you are keenly interested in something, time passes quickly. When you are bored, it drags. When you are expecting someone, it seems forever. When he or she arrives, the moments fly. Time passes much more slowly for children who are looking forward to Christmas than for the adults who are busily preparing for it. Time, in other words, seems relative, even for you. For us it *is* relative, and no question about it.

Ordinarily those of us who are enlightened are unaware of the passing of time. It does not concern us because we have no need for it. The world in which we live does not depend upon the earth's revolving around the sun, or the illusion of day and night, because there is no reason for us to be so oriented. This makes it possible for us to continue to live forever without time having anything to do with it. I know it is difficult for you to think of living forever. You envision an eternity of passing days as impossible to endure. This situation does not arise with us. We just *are*. We're busy and happy and we know we will continue to be, and the element of time does not enter into it.

Yet again, for those whose minds are still fastened tightly to earth —who are in what we call an earthbound state—time drags unmercifully. This is part of the hell they endure because of their unwillingness to take the mental steps necessary to get out of it.

For those of us who are emancipated, however, when time is specifically concentrated on for a special reason, we are able to use it to advantage. Let me illustrate this by the simple account of guardian angels. For at least a while during our development all of us will choose some person still on earth whom we champion. As part of our own soul growth we work with him and send him creative and positive thoughts, thus attempting to make existence more advantageous for him whenever it is in our power to do so. And we do actually, if somewhat whimsically, call ourselves "guardian angels."

If we are working closely with this person we are "guarding," perhaps we go through the events of his day-by-day life with him, and therefore we are involved with time as it affects him. But when he is sleeping at night, it is not necessary for us to be there. We will keep one area of our thoughts attuned to him so that should he awaken and need us, we can be with him, but otherwise we may be spatially at a distance from him and going about our own pursuits. Since we do not need to sleep, we can accomplish a great deal for our own development and entertainment while the subject of our attention is at rest. The moment he awakens we are with him again, giving him our support in every way possible. So you see, time now affects us as it affects him.

Life here, being in most cases timeless, is therefore much less restricting. Since we have no physical corporality for which to care, we do not have to eat or sleep, so we are not even disturbed by periodic needs that must be met on schedule. We are free of the regimens and exertions of bodies that demand constant attention. Most of your time, on the other hand, is concerned with your bodies, for they must be housed, clothed, fed and kept clean before anything else is done. Then you have to give half your time to sleeping in order to "recharge your batteries," and exercising, dressing and undressing, cooking, sewing, cleaning or else providing the income in order to buy everything you and your family require. One of the best things that happens to us at death is this liberation from physical needs.

We do not have to walk in order to progress from one place to another, or ride in a car or train. We have only to think of ourselves at another place and we are there. We do not have to sail across water or swim in it, although if we should wish to have the pleasure of a dip we could concentrate upon doing so and enjoy it. We do not need to protect ourselves from cold or heat, because they are not necessary conditions in the places where we now reside. It is unbelievably rewarding to be free of all these encumbrances of matter.

I do not wish you to think, however, that we are immaterial beings floating around in a void. We are far from it, especially in our early stages of life in the spirit world. We have our spiritual bodies and we live in them, using them just as we used our physical bodies on earth, but not having to be slaves to them.

It is surprising to you, I am sure, to learn just how much of our lives is similar to our previous existence. This is so that the transition between planes will be gradual enough for us to be able to accept it naturally. It must always be kept in mind that you are the same person the moment after death that you were the moment before. Your consciousness is intact and you are You, nobody else. You have the same attitudes, the same thoughts and memories, the same likes and dislikes and habits. Even if you have been altered by illness, mental disease or senility, your consciousness is intact after death and your personal characteristics will soon return to normal as you go along. You have now left a physical body that is no longer of use to you, and you are going to have to learn how to exist without it. In order for you not to find this so overpoweringly confusing that you are unable to cope, you are permitted by the system to live in your spiritual body in similar conditions to those you previously knew and felt comfortable with, in such close proximity to earth that you can continue to feel at home in your new environment.

COMMENTARY:

In *You Do Take It With You* DeWitt Miller, in his defense of the possibility of having a "second," or spiritual, body, has also hit on a justification for the gradual transition of which James speaks: "If we accept our survival of bodily death as proved—a conclusion which seems inescapable—then the second body is logically necessary to maintain an unbroken evolutionary chain. The very heart of evolutionary theory is the conception that progress does not take place by sudden radical changes, but rather by steady and unbroken development. That the process which developed man from the amoeba and the mature individual from the infant—always by a gradual progression—should suddenly make a wild, drastic change, a change completely beyond our conception, seems highly improbable.

"Yet that is just what would occur if we survived death without a body. The process which created us by evolution would on the instant change us into 'disembodied spirits,' entities so foreign to our understanding as to be incomprehensible. The second body seems to me the only reasonable link between worlds.

"Again, if we accept the evidence for survival, the second body is essential for any meaningful conception of the next phase of life following earthly existence. A heaven peopled with disembodied spirits has always defied understanding. Not only is such a hereafter uninteresting, it is inconceivable. The second body is a firm basis on which we can begin to construct some intelligent outline of our next stage of existence."

If an individual is prepared for the fact that there is no precipitate transition from living on earth to living in the next dimension and that the adaptation to the life of spirit is a gradual one, he is better able to accept it when it happens to him. We have always thought that if we lived at all after death, we would have to be entirely transformed immediately. We expected, if anything at all, a change of conditions so vast as to put us into an altogether different circumstance. When this does not occur, we are confused and find it difficult to accept. I must make it clear now that this transition is gradual for a very definite reason. Supreme Intelligence planned it that way as the most sensible and workable arrangement for man's advancement.

What is to come is good, remember that. God's plan for mankind seems to you very difficult as you endure life's traumas; but the overall scheme is wise, and each step is planned so that evolutionary progression is successful. Do not fear change as it comes. Keep your hearts and your minds open and ready for exciting new adventures. I'll guarantee you will have them.

IV
THE CLOSED MIND
AND WHERE IT GETS YOU

THE EXPECTATION OF an abrupt alteration into some amorphous spiritual state entirely different from anything they have ever known frequently makes people unable to understand what has happened to them when death occurs. For those who believe that when one dies he immediately soars into a eudaemonic heaven or is thrust into a fiery hell—depending upon what he considered to be his moral status at the time—it is a shock instead to find himself right where he was and in what seems at first to be the identical situation.

For one who was sure that death was the end of all existence, it is an even greater surprise to find himself still living while at the same time he can see his own body on the bed beside him, or in a car at the scene of a fatal accident, or wherever he died. There are many occasions where such a person refuses to believe what has happened and decides that he is merely having a bad dream. It is possible for such a one to be in this confusion for a long time until he is finally made to realize that he has actually passed from the physical life into the spiritual.

Those who have become aware before they die of the truth about conditions after death and have prepared themselves by learning to live in an acceptably informed manner will find themselves very much better equipped for the new life than persons who were unaware of the fact that they will survive. Those who have closed their minds to the possibility of life after death, or who have led sordid, miserable existences will be completely baffled by the state in which they discover themselves. It may take them a long, long time before they become aware of their potentiality and begin to make some effort to be receptive to new concepts.

One of the biggest pleasures when you first die is to meet and greet old friends and relatives. What they tell you about their conditions will depend upon their state of development and the other spirits with whom they have associated since they came over. If a man's mother, for instance, has done nothing since but hang around his earthly home and try to run his life for him, she will have no new outlook. If his father, on the other hand, has traveled widely among wise spirits, he will explain the facts of Evolutionary Soul Progression—even though that name may not be used for the philosophy he describes—and he will make every effort to start his son on his way immediately, telling him exultantly that his change from physical existence has been the greatest thing that could happen to him and that his hopes for the future are unlimited. Such a relative or friend will be his greatest source of inspiration as he begins his development in the spirit world. If he knows no one already passed over, he will find himself greeted by strangers who make it their business to welcome newcomers in order to lend a hand where necessary.

Many who die have already formed definite opinions as to what life will be like after "passing through the portals." Fundamentalist Christians expect to be welcomed by one no less imposing than Saint Peter himself to usher them through the Pearly Gates. If they find instead only relatives and friends and those spirit helpers who always attempt to greet new arrivals, they will feel neglected. If those who have preceded them were as rigid in their biblical interpretations as they, it is likely that nothing but unhappiness has been their lot since death. They will tell them that the wait for recognition of their virtues has been a long one, that no saints or angels have come to them, and that they are very sad. (Since befriending spirits do not have wings, they have not been recognized by these literal-minded people for the angels of mercy they actually are.) If the truth is not couched in the language expected by this orthodox new arrival, if he is told he must now start to work on his progression, he will not believe. He is supposed to be in heaven already and to see the face of God because he was a good church-going Christian on earth and accepted Jesus Christ as his Savior. Very likely he will think the uplifting spirits who try to tell him the truth are really demons in disguise and will pay no attention to them.

Biblical adherents who are convinced they must sleep until the Day of Resurrection will undoubtedly continue to sleep after death. Some of those who died a long time ago are still slumbering. They will eventually wake up—someone will blow a trumpet to get them up, if nothing else—and then perhaps they will listen to the truth: that their physical bodies will never be resurrected but that their minds must be resurrected from their misconception and started on the right path to development.

Closed minds, no matter whether closed on the subject of the physical resurrection of the body, heaven, hell, nirvana, or oblivion, will get one nowhere in the spirit world. It is best to die prepared for challenging new experiences, and then whatever comes will be accepted with equanimity.

Life after death is as individual an undertaking as life is on earth, and you are on your own just as much as you ever were. There are certain procedures one must follow as he begins his advancement in the next world, and these can be learned from those enterprising spirits you will find all about—whose goals are to uplift their fellows. If you do not listen to them, that is your business. Nobody can force you to do anything. There are no police or truant officers around here to keep you in line when you stray from accepted procedures, and there are no rulers of any kind. There are not even rules on our plane, except the rules of courtesy, love, good will, and accepted behavior. No one, then, can change your character or your personality except yourself. You do not arrive at the feet of Saint Peter or anyone else who will judge you, scold or applaud you, and make everything all right for you. You have instead to choose your own paths and make your decisions just as you always did.

You have the help of teachers and guides who can give you assistance, if you will take it; but you are no more likely to listen to them after your death than you were to listen to guidance on earth. If you were the kind of a person who could never be told anything, you will still be that kind of person. If you knew all the answers on earth, you will still think you do in the next life and will continue to be the same as you always were until you finally begin to realize that you are getting nowhere. Then, out of pure boredom or misery, you will listen to those who state the facts and you will begin to absorb some of their wise council and apply it. Continuing from that point upward becomes a fascinating and enjoyable process and you will rush into it. Opening the mind to new ideas is difficult for most people of an obtuse nature; but once the new thought has been received, nothing can stop their upward progress.

For everyone who dies into waiting arms, there is someone who has so lived that he has no loved friends on the other side. Some persons have even been repudiated by their parents and relatives because of the unpleasantness of their characters and the lives they have led. These are the ones who need help the most, and spirit assistants will from time to time attempt to tell them the truth. Unfortunately, because they find themselves in the identical conditions in which they died, many are not likely to believe what has happened to them, no matter what they are told. It is difficult to convince them they do not now have physical bodies because the bodies in which they find themselves appear to them to be the same ones they had. They do not realize that the substance of their forms is now so composed as to be invisible to those on earth, and so when they are unseen by those with whom they continue to associate, they think they are being ignored. This quite naturally convinces them they are merely having a bad dream. I will give you an example of this from my own experience.

When I died, I was greeted by my parents and told the truth of my condition and soon learned that I must begin to work on my character development. It has been a great effort and I am still working; but I know that eventually I will achieve my goals of perfection, as do all men once they set their feet on the proper path. I have since made it my practice to greet each of my old friends at the moment of his passing and to help indoctrinate him properly about his new condition. I have also been at the deathbed of many who have had no friends to receive them. They have sometimes looked upon me as an intruder who had no business to be there, and when they feel this way there is little I can do to help them.

Picture, if you will, the situation of one whom we will call John Jones because that is not his real name. John Jones had lived a sordid life. His main interests were the attainment of money and the spending of it on himself. He was not always honest, although he could hardly have been called a criminal type. He was successful in his business dealings and at the time of his death was a wealthy man. He was also an uninformed man who did not believe in anything except the power of money and his own ability to make it. He lived well, had a wife and children who endured him and spent his money gladly but had no real affection for him, as he had little for them. His relatives who had died had long ago given him up as one they could not influence for the better, and so they made no effort to stay with him and help him. When this man died suddenly of a heart attack, no one was there to receive him. I heard of his death, and, having known him briefly in life, I decided to try to make his entry into the new phase of his existence as comfortable as possible. I went to greet him.

John Jones was looking down at the figure on the hospital cot, standing beside it with no understanding of what had occurred. I walked up to him and he saw me and gave me a perfunctory greeting. Then he lost interest in me immediately. He was puzzled because that body on the bed looked like him, yet he was standing there feeling better than he had in years, if a bit hazy of mind because of his abrupt demise.

I told him he'd had a sudden heart attack and died. He paid absolutely no attention. I repeated this several times, but he did not listen. Then finally he said, "Look, friend, I'm having a crazy dream. I know exactly what is going on, so please stop bothering me. I have many business deals to put through in the morning and have no time for such silly talk about death."

I gave up trying to impress him with the truth of his situation and merely stood by and watched as he went through his days. His body was taken to the undertakers. When his wife paid it a visit, Jones followed her home. There everything was quieter than usual, his wife and children sitting around taking telephone calls and receiving visitors who came to express regrets. Once in a while Jones looked at me and said, "This is really a weird dream. I wish I could wake up." Even after he had watched his own burial, however, he did not accept the fact that he was dead.

The day after his funeral Jones went to the stock exchange and stayed, as was his wont, watching the rise and fall of stocks as avidly as he had ever done. This went on day after day. I found that I could give him no assistance, so I soon left him, sitting in his office or at the stock market, attempting to advise his fellow workers even though no one was aware of his presence. I checked back on him from time to time and always found him in this same situation. He told me he was getting bored with this silly dream, but he would not listen when I gave him the truth. Death had to be so different from life that this could not be death, and so he must be dreaming. That was the only explanation he would consider.

If we multiply John Jones' experience by the thousands and even millions who so live that their interests are entirely earthly and in no way spiritual, you will see that the sphere immediately after death is burdened with those who should be learning and progressing but instead are tied to the lives they formerly led.

If anyone were to have told Jones' former partners and business associates that they were now being influenced by Jones from the spirit world, they would laugh scornfully. They were sure their own hunches and their knowledge of their professions were sufficient to account for their every instinctive move of buying and selling. Yet the fact that John Jones watched over their shoulders and frequently (if inaudibly) shouted in their ears, "Buy, buy, now's the time" or "Sell, don't be caught in the decline that's coming" probably influenced many a deal. Jones may not have known any more about the situation than the man he was influencing, and his advice may or may not have been correct; but his interest and his strongly projected thoughts penetrated the minds of his associates whether or not they were aware of it.

A wise spirit who is able to see all sides of a question from his vantage point of invisibility can often give helpful advice. Even Jones, who could now read the minds of all the people concerned in a business transaction, would know more about it than the mortals who were involved. Therefore, advice from the spirit world can sometimes be very valuable. But also, if Jones were filled with hate and continually advised someone to do something unethical, the individual might eventually find himself acting against his better judgment. So you can see that spirit influence can be very harmful on occasion. It is unfortunate that those who die in an unenlightened state are most likely to attempt to exert their influence, negative as it is. Those still on earth who are receptive to them may, therefore, be led by them into wrong or inadvisable deeds. The humans who are influenced have no idea they are being coerced from another world when they make mistakes by following what they think is their own intuition.

I can only say here what I will elaborate on more fully at another place: To be forewarned is to be forearmed. If you know the truth of this situation, you will be able to avoid the influences you do not desire; but you will also be able to make use of benevolent spirit help when it is available to you.

It is so easy for sophisticated moderns to toss off anything pertaining to spirit influence as balderdash because there is no scientific evidence of repeatable experiments to verify it. If the amount of money expended on efforts to blast man off the face of the earth were spent on attempts to prove survival, there would be enough evidence to satisfy even the most hardened skeptic. All that is needed is psychic people with enough time and funding for experimentation and a group of objective but sympathetic investigators. If certain mediumistic or strongly psychic persons were subsidized by governmental or other funds so that most of their hours could be given to developing their abilities to communicate, and if these were properly supervised by technicians with an intelligent appreciation of what they were doing, proof of life after death could be achieved within a few years' time. I wish it were possible to convince everyone that billions of dollars spent on weapons and on fantastic schemes of destruction could better be used to learn how to live wisely on earth and how to die in a state of enlightenment. If the facts of survival after death were truly understood, the preservation of every individual would have value to you, no one would be expendable in wars, and the genuine importance of each man would be realized.

Wars, you must know, do not kill a man; they only change him into an invisible enemy. Capital punishment does not get rid of a criminal, it only unleashes him in an unseen form to prey on the world in an even more harmful way.

When Evolutionary Soul Progression is accepted, death will not be such a difficult experience for those who are not ready for it. It is absolutely necessary that you become aware that how a person lives on earth indicates how he will exist after death, and so it is important that each individual live a life of worth to himself and his neighbors. When he does this, he will die in a harmonious state, which will enable him immediately to begin his advancement. When he does not, he will be "earthbound" for a long time.

Being earthbound is the worst possible thing that can happen to one. It is truly a condition of hell and is so tragic that much effort is being spent from my side to try to get the word to those on earth who are in danger of dying without any awareness of their spiritual nature. You people, too, can help by giving this information to all who are potential earthbound spirits. You can also assist by praying for those who die without proper preparation. If you pray for them for a few months after their demise, you will show them that somebody cares, and this should help them get through a most difficult time. Trance mediums who have "rescue circles" have received clear indication that the thoughts of earthbound spirits are so focused onto earth that they will listen to you when they will not listen to us in their own plane.

Had someone been praying for John Jones, there is the possibility that he might have begun sooner to realize that he was in the spirit world. As it turned out, it was not until all his business associates had died, one by one, and he had gone to their funerals and then found them greeting him after their transition, that he finally accepted the fact of his death. Then it was a long time before he began to do anything about improving his lot.

Life after death, when experienced properly from the outset, is so challenging and so marvelously engrossing that life on earth is nothing in comparison. I can truthfully say that when you come to this sphere, you will find so much to interest and excite you that I cannot make it sound attractive enough. But you have to keep your mind open when you arrive in order to get started off properly and save yourself much wasted time, just as you have to keep your mind alert to new ideas and new opportunities on earth. The person with a closed mind, who will not allow any fresh concepts to enter his philosophy, will have a more deplorable time after death than he did on earth. He will have it, that is, until he wakes up and starts his advancement. That is inevitable.

V

INFORMATION ABOUT THE HUMAN MIND

NATURAL LAWS, which govern all of the universe, do not change. You can use them even if you do not know what they are or how they operate. A good example of this is the force called electricity. Now, the Power of Thought is a natural law little understood or accepted by you people at the present time. Yet thought power is the strongest force in the world, and the sooner you accept this truth and put it into practice, the sooner you will benefit from it.

All matter can be controlled by thought, on earth and everywhere else in the universe. If I had said this to you a century ago, you would have scoffed. But now the atom has been split and found to be composed largely of space and energy. Nothing but an infinitesimal amount of matter is discovered within the preponderance of space in each tiny atom; and this infinitesimal amount of matter is described by scientists as energy, force, or power.

COMMENTARY:

Pierre Teilhard de Chardin says in The Phenomenon of Man, *p. 42: "Though never found in a state of purity . . . energy nowadays represents for science the most primitive form of universal stuff."*

The relationship between matter and thought is so obscure to you that it is difficult to explain how thought can affect matter. But it can be done if you will bear with me. I must first remind you that matter, while giving the illusion of solidity, is not actually solid. The nucleus of energy and the particles that move around it provide what might be called a force field of sorts, which gives the manifestation of density. But if these particles were moving at a faster rate of speed, they would not seem dense.

As an example of what I mean: If you throw a baseball slowly, it can be seen passing through the air. If it were projected at an incredible speed, it would be invisible. Or take the blades of a fan or an airplane propeller: When moving slowly, they are visible. But when they are revved up to a high speed, you can see right through them.

Although it is not easy for your doctors to believe this because they have found no evidence of it, the spiritual body within the physical is composed of the same force or energy as all other matter, but it is moving faster than the forces you have so far been able to identify within the atoms.

Now, thought, the strongest force in the world, is another form of energy, and it is strong enough to control the energy in matter. It can be done only by those who know how to concentrate powerfully, but it *can* be done. In our planes of existence it *must* be done, because it is only by the power of our thoughts that we can have anything to use. We must make it for ourselves by thinking forcefully enough to produce it. This is an applying of one force against another, and the stronger causes the manifestation. If you beam your thought consciously, with enough determination, at any object, you can cause it to move or to change in form . . . or to dematerialize and then rematerialize in another location.

COMMENTARY:
When this was originally written, there had been few actual tests to prove the power of mind over matter, except for the dice-throwing experiments done in Dr. Rhine's Parapsychology Laboratory at Duke and the reports that had come from certain séances back in the days of such great physical mediums as Eusapia Palladino and D. D. Home. These latter researches, while startling in their import if true, were always open to question because of the difficulty in controlling conditions to such an extent that the integrity of the participants might not be questioned.

Today, however, although people who know how to influence physical objects by the power of their minds are by no means prevalent, there are several who are actually being tested in lighted laboratories under controlled conditions. Their ability to use their minds to move objects (called psychokinesis or PK) or in other ways to modify or alter physical substance is now a matter of record.

In the USSR Nina Kulagina by concentration has caused the movement of a wide range of nonmagnetic objects: large crystal bowls, clock pendulums, bread, matches, a cigar tube, a salt cellar and other things. In one test a raw egg was placed in a salt solution inside a sealed aquarium six feet away from Kulagina. Researchers report she was able to use PK to separate the yolk from the white of the egg. I have seen movies of her in the process of causing the movements of objects and they reveal her to become intensely emotional as she exerts a tremendous amount of mind power. In fact the reports show that her blood sugar and endocrine measurements reveal her to be in a state of controlled rage.

Today in the United States two psychics who are able to cause movement of or changes in objects by the power of their thought are being studied by the Stanford Research Institute think tank. Neither is as personally dramatic about it as Kulagina; neither gets into such an emotional tizzy as she does. But their results are just as spectacular.

Ingo Swann, in an experiment conducted by Dr. Gertrude Schmeidler at New York's City College, was able to effect temperature changes in graphite thermistors at a distance or, in other words, to make a small piece of graphite become hotter or cooler when it was from three to ten feet away from him. At the Stanford Institute, using a shielded magnetometer, Swann demonstrated "an ability to increase and decrease at will the magnetic field within a superconducting magnetic shield," according to Psychic, April, 1973.

A twenty-six-year-old Israeli sensitive named Uri Geller has used his mind to produce similar phenomena under controlled conditions at Stanford Institute. He is not afraid to perform in front of large crowds and has shown his powers on nationwide television on several occasions. On the Jack Paar Show and the Merv Griffin Show, while someone else was holding the object and one or two of his fingers were barely touching it, he has caused railroad spikes to bend and a ring to break in half.

Astronaut Captain Edgar Mitchell has observed Geller a number of times, and he says in Psychic: *"In addition to the rigidly controlled experimental work that has been done with Uri Geller . . . there are many startling events that take place when he is around and in the proper state of mind. An evening with Geller is likely to produce an assortment of bent rings, bent and broken silverware, mysteriously lost articles and mysteriously found articles. . . . For example, it is not unusual to see Uri pick up a normal spoon to stir his coffee and have the spoon come out of the coffee twisted or broken. . . . On one particular evening, approximately twenty such bizarre events . . . took place in less than three hours, in the presence of three well-qualified observers."*

Although we often think of man primarily as his body, his consciousness is actually the reality—the man himself. The physical body is only the material mechanism in which the spiritual body and the consciousness live. The mind is not identical with the brain, as materialists have been inclined to maintain. Mind is an overall word that includes the concepts of soul or spirit or consciousness and unconsciousness; and the brain is the physical mechanism through which it operates. There is no enclosed space anywhere in existence labeled "mind." The mind is, rather, a complex of forces, which like the spiritual body surround and interpenetrate the physical body.

The consciousness is the aspect of the mind that is aware of itself —the "I-thinker" (to use Professor Hornell Hart's phrase). The fact that your consciousness seems to you to be within your head, usually at the center of the forehead between your eyes, is because that is the point at which the mind expresses conscious awareness through the physical body. When you are awake, it is because the consciousness is focusing through this area of your brain. When you are asleep or unconscious, your consciousness, while still operating in and about the physical organism, is not projecting itself through the center of awareness.

The mind is said to be divided (but it is not really divided at all— there are no levels or layers of the human mind) into the conscious, the unconscious and the superconscious. We can say that these are all aspects of the mind, and we will use the terms as a convenience even though they are not exactly accurate.

The superconscious is actually no more than the conscious mind when it is most highly motivated and spiritually attuned, and at its most psychic. It could be referred to as the soul.

The subconscious is, among other things, the aspect of the mind that controls all bodily functions. It is expressed throughout both the spiritual and the physical bodies, operating in every cell and in every organ. The subconscious is also the storehouse of memories. The subconscious does not think, and when it is in control of the body, as when one is asleep, heavily hypnotized, or in a deep state of trance, the body may talk and move about, but no actual thinking is going on . . . unless some visiting spirit is in possession of the body. The subconscious is also each mortal's contact with the universal subconscious.

This concept of a universal subconscious, and even the idea of Akashic Records, are partial glimpses of the truth, for there is what might be called an Astral image of everything that ever occurs. Past events, even sometimes those of little significance, can be sensed occasionally when proper conditions prevail and psychic persons are involved. Dramatic events in which great emotion was expended are perceived rather frequently. When psychic individuals tap historical data from these memory banks, people are frequently under the impression that they are recalling past lives. Access to such knowledge is also a form of extrasensory perception known as "retrocognition."

Sights or sounds of old battles have sometimes been witnessed or heard; demolished houses are seen still standing on occasion. Murders are sometimes observed being reenacted in haunted houses. This does not mean that the spirits of the murderer and murdered are continually repeating the scene. It is instead because a highly emotional event makes such a strong impression on the atmosphere that it is, you might almost say, photographed there.

Willpower does not rule over the subconscious, for the principle governing it is suggestion. Just try willing yourself to remember something you have forgotten and see how far you get. When you want to recall a thing to mind, suggest to your subconscious that it can find the name or memory of which you are in need. Allow it to root around and locate the information while you occupy your outer consciousness with something else. Sooner or later the right answer will pop into your mind. You can will yourself to think and to act, but it is impossible to force the subconscious mind.

Consciousness can withdraw its attention at any time and the body continues to operate without it, as in sleep, unconsciousness, trance or coma. The conscious awareness may on occasion actually leave the body and exist independently of it as is illustrated in many cases of out-of-the-body travel. But the moment the subconscious leaves, the body dies.

Memories contain the reactions of the individual to each and every thought, sensation, movement, perception, and action that is in any way impressed on the mind or body. Memories are intact after death and available when sought. Because of this, the mind is complete and useful in every way after death. Your capability during life is sometimes thought to be hampered by the fact that all memories are not immediately available, but this is actually a protective measure. If they were handy at all times, they would be too impressive and you would find it impossible to sort out what you wanted from all the residue.

After death the power of the mind becomes more obvious, but if you would learn to use it more while you are on earth, you would have much greater success in all your efforts to cope with life. No one need be sick if he knows how to concentrate properly on health. No one need be poor or miserable no matter how hopeless his case may seem. Make yourself use this power as consistently as possible, religiously attempting the techniques I will give in the next chapter. You should practice positive thinking as diligently as you would practice the violin if you desired to become a virtuoso.

VI

HOW TO USE YOUR THOUGHTS EFFECTIVELY

THOSE WHO WISH to live so that they will have more success on earth and a head start in future planes of existence have only to decide to live that way. When you make up your mind that you will expend the effort to keep your life in a constructive path and maintain your thoughts under control, you can learn to do so. While it is very hard work, it is not a great deal more difficult than to give up a bad habit or to learn a new capability.

The way you think can affect your body as quickly as germs can, making it ill if you have become angry too easily and too often, or if you have hated too much, or if you have despaired or feared too much. Hatred held strongly will cause disease and decay in your body. There is no cure for hating except positive action taken to change your way of thinking so that you will learn to love. Natural laws are in operation here as everywhere else. If you wish to change your thinking from negative to positive, you must consciously apply the law of Thought Power positively. Whenever you find yourself thinking negatively, deny the negative thought and substitute a positive one in its place. This is the way the law works, and when you learn how to use it you will reveal corresponding success in your life.

COMMENTARY:

In Self-Realization *magazine, summer, 1973, was this little gem:*

"If you want to drive darkness out of a room, you don't use a flyswatter and keep hitting at the darkness, do you? Because even if you could do that a thousand years, you would not drive it away. The way to drive darkness out of the room is to turn on the light, or strike a match. The way to overcome your negative thinking is to apply the opposite, positive thinking."

Consciousness controls everything. All matter, which is composed of energy in a constant state of activity, is directed by mind, the overall regulating principle of the system through which it functions. If you consistently think positive, constructive thoughts, your life will reflect it. And you will also feel well; for your entire anatomy tends to operate normally. Negative thoughts cause the opposite reaction. So keep yourself in top condition by thinking happy thoughts and not causing your cells conflict.

You can cure illnesses by the proper positive thinking because when you firmly believe that you are well, your body is motivated to begin to act that way. Watch yourself over a period of time and see if this is not true. There is nothing more effective for good than the constructive thoughts held strongly in your mind.

COMMENTARY:

Some physicians are beginning to realize this today. For instance, Air Force Major O. Carl Simonton, MD, a radiation therapist and cancer specialist and Director of Radiology at Travis Air Force Base in California, is thoroughly convinced that one's state of mind has a lot to do with the development of cancer and must be reckoned with in treating it as well. In a lecture I attended, he said, "The mind, the emotions, and the attitude of a patient play a role in both the development of a disease, cancer included, and the response that a patient has to any form of treatment."

Thus, in addition to being treated with cobalt radiation, Dr. Simonton's patients learn meditation and are involved in psychotherapy, and some of them are benefiting tremendously from it. He has found that a direct correlation exists between the attitude of the patient and the response of the patient's cancer to therapy. Dr. Simonton postulates that in some way the condition of the mind lowers "host resistance" to malignant cells. "The immunological defenses, mostly concentrated within the white cells of the blood and *lymph systems, fail to do their usual job and allow the cancer to grow,"* he says. *And the mind must have an influence on the immunological responses.* He recalls that as far back as the 1950's "researchers in immunology found that host resistance to the bacillus which caused tuberculosis was affected by the patient's psychological state."

During his speech at the Academy of Parapsychology and Medicine Symposium in Oakland, California, in June 1973, Dr. Simonton stated *"our thoughts, our attitudes, our minds, our emotions play a very significant role in development of diseases and our bodies' responses to them."* It was the study of biofeedback and mind-training courses that gave him the meditative techniques he has learned to use as a combination of relaxation and visualization, showing him that it was possible to put under conscious control those bodily processes not normally under conscious control. In addition, his patients and their families are educated about their cancers and what they need to do, and they participate in three-times-a-week psychotherapy groups, open to all family members or others important to the patient.

Dr. Simonton shows his lecture audiences slides of lesions in their initial stages and then as they improved when the patient began to formulate some personal framework to get them under control according to his suggested techniques. He would instruct the patients to take no more than fifteen minutes three times a day for deep breathing and muscle relaxation. Then, as described in Psychic (August, 1973), the patient would picture his cancer the way it seemed to him and then *"visualize the army of white blood cells coming in, swarming over the cancer, and carrying off the malignant cells which have been weakened or killed by the barrage of high energy particles of radiation therapy given off by the cobalt machine, the linear accelerator, or whatever the source is."* These white cells break down the malignant cells, which are then flushed out of the body. Finally, just before the end of the meditation, the patient visualizes himself well.

The slide pictures reveal the body's tremendous ability to repair itself, the response being definitely related to the attitude of the patients. If they were fully cooperative and enthusiastic, there was marked relief of symptoms in a short period of time. Those less highly motivated had considerably slower results or none at all.

Dr. Simonton recommends manipulation of attitudes for all cancer patients. "They should get in touch with themselves and with God," he stated.

The power of mind is more forceful than any other power on earth. I do not mean this to be interpreted as it has so often been in the past, that men can think of something, as an architect designs a building, and then with his hands and lumber construct it. I mean that he accomplishes it by using the actual force he is able to generate with his thoughts. In other words, it is possible by powerful thinking, great emotion and faith to cause objects to move, disappear, or even be built up of matter. No man living on your earth has ever fully understood this as much as Jesus Christ did. He was so thoroughly aware of it that he could make loaves and fishes appear in quantity for a multitude, change water into wine, heal the sick, and even walk on water. There is no reason to doubt these stories, because he was demonstrating a law that has worked to a lesser extent for others before and since. There is no reason that everyone could not do this, if he understood fully how to concentrate and had sufficient faith in his ability.

Even when the conscious mind is paying attention to certain bodily functions that are usually left entirely to the subconscious, as when you are intent upon deep breathing or exercising certain muscles, the subconscious proceeds normally in other areas, such as keeping the blood flowing and the heart beating. It never once relaxes until you die. Because the body responds to what either aspect of the mind tells it to do, the consciousness must be careful what it puts into the subconscious as emotion-laden memories. If you hate someone bitterly or hold thoughts of despair and discouragement, they are placed on record in the subconscious storehouse (as well as in the universal unconscious). When a large amount of discord is stored there, it begins to react on the body in a negative manner. Your glands and organs register the kind of activity needed to combat anguish. In other words, they send out secretions or become overactive in order to repair the negative condition. When your organs do not function normally, you become ill. It may not happen immediately, but persisted in over a period of time, negative thinking will cause illness. You see, if illness or tension comes, your cells immediately start to combat them by unusual activity. If your body is told constantly by your emotions to overact and overexert itself to combat conditions caused by hatred and fear and misery imprisoned within the subconscious mind, it will do so. Many aspects of bodily function can be changed by your thinking, and you can be sick or well because of it. Do not doubt this for one moment.

Your body wants to do what you tell it. Your consciousness is the master of the mechanism through which it operates. It has to be obeyed, and it is obeyed, even though sometimes the results are the opposite of what you actually wish. Keep your body well and happy by thinking happy thoughts and not causing your cells conflict. You can cure illness by the proper positive thinking; because when you firmly believe that your body is well and happy, it is motivated to begin to act that way. Watch yourself over a period of time and see if this is not true. There is nothing more effective than the constructive thoughts you hold strongly in your mind.

Certainly I know that this is not easy when you are in physical pain or discomfort. That is why it is wise to start your constructive program when you are young and healthy. Yet even those of you in whom negative thought patterns are already established can benefit by consciously applied effort to counteract them. If you do not want to be sick, start every day with the statement that you are a brilliant, stimulating mind living in a healthy, normally functioning body. Let no negative reaction deny this as the day goes forward, and occasionally repeat the statement. Of course, I know that if you are in actual physical pain this is not easy. Some pain can be minimized by proper thinking about it, rejecting it and forbidding it to hurt. Some pain is more difficult to control. Yet when another person holds proper thoughts about you, sometimes your painful illnesses can be relieved or completely eliminated. This is why Christian Scientists sometimes go to practitioners when they become ill. They know that the power of their own thoughts is not strong enough to overcome such a distressful situation in which they are closely involved. They also know that the power of a person trained professionally to deny the reality of the existence of illness and pain is able to have its effect on them. Much of what is taught by Religious Science, Christian Science, Unity, and other sects that utilize the power of thought to maintain successful living is correct and helpful. I recommend joining with others in religious organizations that have the control of the mind as their main object. It will reinforce your interest in attempts to improve yourself. The same kind of positive thinking can be applied individually, however, and it is necessary if you are to have a properly ordered life.

If you would teach your small children, as soon as they learn to speak, to start each day with an aphorism of health and happiness, their lives would be much more successful in every way. The child should learn to say each morning as soon as he opens his eyes: "Today I will be healthy and happy all day long." Nothing else is necessary. He must learn to say it, not as a rote, but as an affirmation as important in the morning as his prayer at night. If he begins with this very early, even before he can talk plainly, it will be such a part of his life's patterns that he will not think of it as a chore but as a normal routine. His life will be immeasurably improved because of it.

Positive thinking, unless it is learned from childhood, is never easy, and sometimes it takes a great deal of conscious work in order to keep your mind from dwelling on negatives. To learn to control your thinking is one of the most difficult lessons of life; but it is essential that you know it. There are many times when it will be all you can do to keep from saying a cross word, to stop feeling sorry for yourself, or to lift your morale when it is low. Effort is needed; but if you will expend the effort over a period of time, you will find that it has been worthwhile. It cannot be easy to gain control over thinking habits that have been allowed to persist without discipline all your life. But constant effort to keep them in check for a while will force your thoughts to follow your wishes, and then you will see that your entire existence is correspondingly improved.

Nothing you do to uplift yourself makes any difference unless you think right about it. You may get up every morning and go to church, but if you sit in your pew and grieve or envy someone or go over and over in your mind some insult or rebuff, you might as well have stayed at home.

Positive thinking may be laughed at by those who have not tried it; but the ones who practice it know that it works. They have learned from experience that it changes lives. You may live in physical discomfort and mental disharmony all your life until you learn to think constructively; then everything about your existence will alter for the better. Let no one talk you out of the necessity for positive thinking.

It is also highly important that the power of mass opinion be recognized. Anything strongly believed by a large number of people is a definite force, and it is important that its effect be understood. Whenever one of you goes against public opinion, he is fighting an actual force as great as if he were charging into a battalion of soldiers. It is important that strongly held mass opinions that are wrong be changed, but it requires the efforts of many for long periods of time to do this.

Unless you are very well trained and developed in your youth, you are not likely to learn how to use your thoughts to change or construct physical objects until you have passed through the experience of death. But if you wished to expend enough time and effort on it, you could learn it now. If you have used your thought power well during your life, you will die ahead of the game, knowing already what others will probably take a long time learning. Each person born on earth must eventually develop all his talents and capabilities to their highest degree so that he can grow into the harmonious and wise individual who can ultimately achieve the heights of spiritual development. What is the very first step in this progression? Knowledge of the power of thought.

If you will attempt to make it a practice always to deny a negative thought the moment it appears and immediately substitute a positive one, half your battle will be won. Never for any period of time let your thoughts wander aimlessly on negative aspects of life. Alert yourself immediately to the fact that you are not only wasting time but forming and maintaining bad thought patterns. Start deliberately to concentrate upon something pleasant instead. Never allow yourself to dwell on a hurt or a worry. If your mind won't leave it, get very busy at any job you may have to do or take a walk, play the piano, read a book, watch television—do anything that will take your mind off it.

If someone has said something offensive to you, you can go over and over it in your mind until it looms as large as a thunderhead. Or you can repress it, saying, "I won't think about that. I won't. I won't. It was a terrible thing for him to say and I'll never, never forgive him; but I mustn't think about it." This will record a number of unpleasant concepts in your subconscious mind for possible future effects. Do not repress the unpleasant problem by giving it so much power, for that will push it down into your subconscious as if it were something important requiring action. Instead, dismiss it casually and substitute a positive thought for it immediately. Think, as lightly as possible, "That was bad, all right, but he's probably sorry now that he said it. Anyway, I know I didn't deserve it." Of course, if you realize you did deserve the criticism you received, accept it, learn from it, and then dismiss it entirely and go on thinking about other things. Every time you find your thoughts dwelling on the insult again, say, "No, I won't think about it. He's a nice person. I am sure he didn't mean any harm."

You may weary yourself trying to recall kind things to say about him; but you will stop the worrying. And you will be learning how to handle your thoughts. Granted that it will take considerable effort for a long time to learn such mental control. Mind training is not easy. But it is so well worth the trouble that it should be the first rule of operation you learn in life.

COMMENTARY:
I think of James' advice so often when I read the news and watch television. I have learned from him never to read the reports about wars, for I tend to get upset over them. Being a news enthusiast, I know what is going on, but do not let myself concentrate on the depressing information any more than I can help. I know some people whose days are actually miserable because the price of beef has gone up or the political situation is not to their liking or there is more fighting in Ireland. I used to be one of them.

The same thing should be done with commercials. Whenever I see some housewife crooning "poor baby" to a husband who is grousing about his drippy nose or headache, I deny its applicability to me. I actually say aloud at that moment, "I do not want a cold and will not get one." There is little doubt that incessantly repeated advertising of such a contrary nature is being unwittingly accepted by many persons who say to themselves, "Oh, that's just the way I feel. I must be coming down with a cold." And then they do come down with a cold. It is very important that the people of the world learn to fight the constant negatives that are being thrown at us by our media by replacing them with positive thoughts.

Making the best of everything is the only way to live. Those who always consider the worst of it keep themselves unhappy and unsuccessful. Back of every rich businessman is a positive knowledge of his abilities and his talents and his goals. He has such self-confidence that he cannot help but win. He knows his place in the sun and he achieves it because of his knowledge. Often his personal life may not be so rewarding as his business life, for he may not be aware of his God-relatedness. If he has that knowledge as well, nothing can stop him from being a winner in everything he undertakes. Those who are aware of their ultimate immortality and their need to think positively at all times are so far ahead of their fellows that their lives always reflect a glow of happiness and success.

VII

THE GRADUAL TRANSITION

WHEN ONE PASSES through the experience called death, he has two alternatives: He may react to our instruction and begin his progression, or he may stay at the level of enlightenment where he already is for any length of time he chooses. If he decides in favor of achievement, his life immediately improves. From that very moment a great weight usually drops from his shoulders. Those who have been especially immoral or insensitive to hurting others will not immediately be happy, for they have so much remorse. When they start to face up to the things they have done wrong and try to right them, they realize that it will take them many years to overcome the problems they have caused. Yet even these spirits, after they have made the decision to take the forward step, are in a better and more pleasant state than they would have been otherwise.

The individual who starts upward is taught so much and has so many things to think about that he is busy every moment. Those who envision heaven as inhabited by doddery old parties sitting around on clouds in their nightshirts strumming harps have a surprise in store. Heaven is a place of enterprise and activity so interesting and constructive as to be a constant challenge. A description of your life in the lower heavenly spheres will show what I mean, as spirits who have just been inspired to begin their advancement get oriented and learn how to cope with existence in the new dimension.

In the first place, you look as you think you deserve to look. Because everything is controlled by thought, you appear to yourself and to others in your own mental image. Those who die as young men and women still envision themselves as youthful (although children grow up in their spiritual bodies in the spirit world). If you had aged and withered, as time has a way of deteriorating us all, you die with an appearance with which you would not wish to continue to exist. So one of the first things you must do when your progression starts is think yourself young again. You will soon begin to feel so well anyway, without the physical body worn by age and illness, that your thoughts about yourself will reflect it; and then your appearance will represent you at your peak of beauty and physical fitness. If you were never beautiful, there is even a good deal you can do to repair that, for the glow of health and happiness can make anyone attractive. Others will then view you as you look to yourself. It is rewarding when you first meet friends over here and see that they have regained their youthful vigor. When you hear them exclaiming that you look as well to them, you are delighted. Enjoyment of the sensations of a body that is always young and healthy is a constant pleasure!

It may be, however, that you prefer to remain as a much more mature individual, believing that you had attained the height of your physical and mental achievement in, say, your fifties. In such a case you would continue to picture yourself at that stage of your development and would appear that way to others.

How you look is of first importance in your progression, because you could not think of yourself as old and ill and still have the positive mental attitude needed to advance. You are told when you are greeted by wise spirits after your death how to get for yourself the necessary appearance you wish to have. Then how to use your thoughts for everything else is explained to you.

On earth, as I have said, the power of thought would be able to materialize objects for you if you knew the correct techniques and used the proper mental effort. In spirit spheres there is no other way for you to get anything except to visualize it for yourself, and so you have to learn how to do it. It is essential to use your thoughts properly or you will not make progress. It is not easy to form an object with your mind power alone; and time and effort are necessary to learn this. If you think about something constantly enough and with enough mental effort, however, you can produce it in front of you.

You are told that you will be able to make for yourself many earth-type objects even though you have passed out of the material phase of existence. This, it is carefully explained, is because your transition will be gradual, and in your transitional stage you will continue to want what you have been familiar with on earth. An abrupt alteration in your life-style and your way of doing things would be difficult for you, and if you were suddenly to become only an essence of some kind, floating about in the atmosphere, you would be completely disoriented. The evolutionary process is always by slow degrees. So in the Etheric you maintain a semblance of the type of reality you had while in the physical body, and you can retain it as long as you wish.

The progressor will soon realize that such earthlike requirements as sleeping, eating and drinking are nonessential; and he begins to learn to get along without them. Until you have accepted this, however, your former routines remain. If you smoked cigarettes, you still want them, so you make yourself a smoke now and then until you break the habit. You may eat if you care to. It is not now necessary for your existence, but for those who enjoy a good meal suddenly not to have one is too big a change. For one who has lived for years on strict diets, it is a great pleasure to whip up a cake or pie or cream puff and eat it with no fear of adding pounds or having a gastric attack.

COMMENTARY:
Such statements as this are bound to cause controversy, even though James has explained the necessity for a gradual transition, which requires that the first dimension after death be so nearly like life on earth. From my first days of research in this field I recall reading snide references to the book Raymond *by Sir Oliver Lodge, just because Raymond said they had cigars in the spirit world. This controversial book was written in 1918 by a very prominent scientist who had become convinced of life after death because he believed he was receiving evidential communications through mediums from his son Raymond, who was killed in the First World War. There is*

very little in the book of a philosophical content, but in a few paragraphs Raymond attempts to tell something about what it is like where he was.

The medium Gladys Osborne Leonard's control Feda gave a message from Raymond as follows: "He wants people to realize that it's just as natural as on the earth plane." She goes on, "He says he doesn't want to eat now. But he sees some who do; he says they have to be given something which has all the appearance of an earth food. People here try to provide everything that is wanted. A chap came over the other day who would have a cigar." Raymond thought nobody in the spirit world would be able to provide that, but, he said through Feda, "There are laboratories over here, and they manufacture all sorts of things in them. . . . It's not the same as on the earth plane, but they were able to manufacture what looked like a cigar." Feda said that Raymond didn't try one himself, because he didn't care to, but the other chap jumped at it. "But when he began to smoke it, he didn't think so much of it; he had four altogether, and now he doesn't look at one. They don't seem to get the same satisfaction out of it, so gradually it seems to drop from them. But when they first come they do want things. Some want meat, and some strong drink; they call for whiskey sodas. Don't think I'm stretching it when I tell you that they can manufacture even that. But when they have had one or two, they don't seem to want it so much—not those that are near here."

Naturally, with no more than this to help us understand the system—Raymond had only been "over" a couple of months then and probably did not know anything more by way of explanation of what was going on—readers, especially scientists, scoffed at the idea of cigars and whiskey sodas in the spirit world and dismissed the whole book as nonsense. I did, too, when I first read it.

It will be noted that Raymond's suggestion that there are factories to produce your cigars for you varies from James' assertion that you make everything for yourself. When I asked about it, James said that such laboratories aren't necessary, but that during wartime the soldiers who die are provided whatever they want at first. Usually, however, if a newcomer desires something, he can ask an enlightened spirit how to go about getting it and be taught how to concentrate to produce it himself.

After you have learned to make things with your thoughts, you may wish to try out your new talent in different ways. Most of us build ourselves houses in which to live, and you may wish to do so, too. You do not really need one anymore, yet many of us like the idea of having homes to which we may repair for contemplation, entertaining guests, and even family life—if we still remain close to those we loved who have also passed on. The dwelling is constructed as carefully and specifically as you would build a house of physical matter; although it is done quite differently. You don't have to imagine yourself sawing boards or nailing them into walls and floors. But you do have to envision the home as it will be when completed, in its entirety, and then conceptualize it bit by bit until it is constructed.

When you work with small objects, you may mentally produce the materials and then actually use your hands to form the finished work if you wish. An artist, for instance, visualizes the oils and turpentine and canvas and brushes and then uses them just as he would on earth. But large buildings are more likely to be made by mental activity alone. The minds and hands of many cooperated to build the magnificent public structures you will see in the higher reaches of the Astral.

So what you end up with for yourself may become a tiny hut or a mansion, depending upon your desires and your abilities to conceive by thought power. Or it might be an exact image of a favorite home of yours on earth. The longer you remain in the spirit world, the greater your abilities are to picture what you desire and find it immediately before you.

Whenever you wish to meet with friends, just send out a call to them mentally. Some of them will surely arrive soon, ready to give you the pleasure of their company for as long as you both wish to spend in conversation. Now, when you are first in the Etheric plane you are very likely to think you must entertain somewhat as you did previously, by feeding your guests, furnishing them with cool drinks or coffee, and perhaps even offering them candy or liquor. Your advanced friends will go along with you and accept your hospitality, although they may have grown to the point where they do not feel the necessity for such indulgences as eating and drinking. You have gone to the trouble of thinking up these things for their diversion, and so they will humor you; but if you had offered them nothing but your companionship, and perhaps shared with them your interesting experiences adjusting to the Astral, they would have been more than satisfied.

COMMENTARY:
Can't you just imagine a group from the same small town visiting together in the home of a friend in the spirit world? I doubt if their conversation would change much from what it might have been on earth. It would probably deal largely with mutual acquaintances both here and there, but from an interestingly different viewpoint:
  "Oh, did you know that Martha Burns is over here now?"
  "Yes, she was ill for a long time, but you should see her now—she looks wonderful!"
  "And what about old Joe Sims? He's been hanging on for so long that his relatives here are getting impatient."
  "I know. It's sad when the spirit is so reluctant to leave the flesh. If he only knew what's in store, he would rush right on over."
  "Won't you have some more of this lemon pie?" asks the hostess. "I made it myself, and believe me, it was the most complicated cooking procedure I ever encountered. Enjoy it, for it's probably the last I'll ever make."

I am sure that it is not easy for some readers to understand that mind alone can produce seemingly physical objects and allow them to be used. Many feel that the spirit world should consist of nothing but advanced souls flying about doing good, or evil men being punished. Yet this is not the true situation here and you might as well understand it now before we go any further. Initially life after death is so much like life on earth that the lack of difference is one of the most startling aspects. The only apparent change at first is that now those with whom you had been existing on earth are no longer aware of your presence. After a brief time, unless you choose to become a guardian to one of them, if you are wise you will leave them to their own pursuits (except at times when they have definite problems with which you can help them), realizing that your interests must be with those advanced souls who can take your mind away from the world of your past and teach you the glories of your future.

Even when you begin to turn your thoughts from the situation in which you formerly existed, you still hold to many of your old ideas and habits. It is not until you move to more advanced planes farther from your planet that your thoughts will leave your old ways almost entirely and you will become less earth-oriented and more spirit-oriented. As you progress away from your earthly home, you become increasingly interested in mental rather than physical pursuits. But any abrupt change into a mystical state would be much more difficult for you, believe me.

Accept, then, my statement that thinking materially while in the Astral plane is not wrong; it is right. Divine Consciousness, which evolved the system of gradual transition, knew exactly what it was doing. Earthly customs and characteristics must be eliminated almost imperceptibly. Very few persons come over here in such an advanced state that they do not continue to desire physical gratifications for some period of time. Even sex still retains its attractions to us in the earlier phases of life in the hereafter. It often happens that the earthbound spirit becomes a voyeur, experiencing earthly pleasures vicariously as he watches. This seldom occurs with those whose thoughts are more elevated.

Persons who love each other, who are reunited after death, for the most part find no need for sexual relations. However, if they wished it, they could experience it. But great love may be shared so exquisitely here that the physical contacts are not really as important as they used to be. Life is so filled with inspiring mental activities that most of the needs of the body fade from your interest within a relatively short while after your progression is under way. Time and development take care of physical wants.

Truly successful marriages on earth usually continue after death; and two lovers who for some reason were not married may wish to become so. But all marriages were by no means made in heaven, nor do they continue there. If no true mental and spiritual union exists, very soon all ties are broken and each partner progresses alone until he may find someone else with whom he feels a vitally close affinity. Couples may progress together, growing constantly more close; other individuals may prefer to remain alone.

The term Soulmates actually means that occasionally there are two persons who feel incomplete without each other. They may continue to remain together as closely as they wish for as long as they wish. Their rapport is a beautiful thing to see. The term does not mean, however, that there are inevitably or even occasionally two people who are each half a person and who will only be complete by physical and spiritual union with each other, or who are required by fate eventually to meld into one individual. This is a complete misconception.

As progression advances, all connections between those who have no truly warm relationships are broken off, usually by mutual consent, and others may be formed or not as the individual sees fit. All who have progressed understand this and make no attempt to cling to those to whom they were tied on earth, unless the feeling is entirely reciprocal. Yes, of course, some will try to hang on to others to whom they were related or married. It will be a sign of their advancement when they are able to release those who desire their freedom. A person who had two or more spouses on earth may choose one of them to continue to be with, or may just remain good friends with both or all of them. As you all advance, all adjustments will be made happily and successfully. The clingers and the hangers-on are the earthbound; but *you* will never be one of those. Death, as you now know, is graduation into something that will be much finer and better than what you have now or anything you are able to envision. Think of it that way.

VIII

THE PLEASURES OF PARADISE

Much has been written about heaven, but I do not think it has ever really been described accurately . . . because it is a condition as much as a place. It is true that one does not begin to achieve it until he attains the higher reaches of the Astral plane, but he gets an insight into its joys from the first moment his progression begins. Beyond the Astral heaven, each sphere is increasingly sublime until Divine Consciousness is finally attained.

The concepts gleaned from biblical references to heaven are so vague as to give an impression of unnatural conditions. And what has been understood as life after death has seemed terribly dull. If one accepted Christianity, even on his deathbed, he was immediately thrust into an impersonal area of vague happiness. Even the nirvana of the occultists—which seems in the main to be a goal of extinction not only of all desires and passions but also of individual existence so that the soul can be absorbed into the Supreme Spirit—has a negativity that does not recommend it to the Western mind.

Instead of all this, the true heavenly states are comprised of ardent, eventful and useful activity. To those to whom work is anathema, this does not sound at all like paradise; but believe me, it is the only way. Indeed, as soon as one begins his progression he also starts to appreciate all the opportunities available to him not only for self-regeneration and service to others, but also for pure pleasure.

It will be noted that I apply the terms "heaven" and "paradise" interchangeably, because it really does not matter which I use. They do not refer to any actual physical places, but only to more advanced conditions of mind. The heavenly state is not a layer of sky we reach as we travel outward from the earth; it is a condition we achieve when we have progressed to a certain point in our development. And it could just as readily be described as paradise.

The length of time it takes a spirit to advance to the heavenly state after he has once put his feet on the upward path differs with each individual. One may be so eager that he endeavors constantly to improve himself so that he will arrive as quickly as possible at the highest reaches of the Astral. Even the happiness of heaven will not hold him for long as, ardently pursuing perfection, he leaves the Etheric and proceeds as rapidly as he can through the higher planes toward achievement of Ultimate Perfection and eternal bliss.

Others are handicapped by their lack of enthusiasm for the effort it will entail to begin their advancement, their satisfaction with the situation in which they already find themselves, their inability to listen to what they must do to progress, or perhaps even their generally earthbound state. Faults such as these can and eventually will be overcome with the help of ministering spirits. Once the laggards realize the delight in opening their minds and starting to respond to all the challenges of heaven, they desperately regret the time they have wasted.

Many who have reported on conditions from this side—either spirits speaking through mediums or those fortunate mortals who have had out-of-body experiences and traveled briefly to spirit dimensions—have spoken of the beauty of the surroundings. It is true that beauty is in the eye of the beholder; but when you begin your progress here, your eyes are opened to all of the magical world around you. It is so overwhelming that you from your earth plane can not possibly believe what we say about the infinite variety of trees, the sparkling streams, the flowers with fragrance and color beyond all imagination. What makes it all so especially wonderful is the love and happiness that is all-pervading.

Someone once wrote an analogy comparing the universe as seen by an enlightened spirit to a great Gothic cathedral. An individual who goes into Notre Dame or Westminster Abbey at night with only a candle may see glimpses of the artistry around him, but he has no possible conception of the magnificence that is actually there. One who looks out onto the universe from your world is like that. In the daytime he sees a sky, sun and clouds. At night he sees a moon and twinkling stars. He does not know that in and around those tiny lights there are all kinds of beauties invisible to human eyes. Here happiness, peace, love, color and music are so intertwined with ravishing vistas that only blissful enjoyment is possible.

You must realize that the visions I am describing are as real and solid as anything you have on earth. They are constructed, it is true, by our thoughts, our imaginings, our dreams—and those of all the millions who have passed before us, plus the spiritual replicas of all the material vistas on all inhabited planets—but they are material nonetheless. Although not technically exact, the best way I can explain it so you will understand is to say that they are composed of force or energy that vibrates at a much higher frequency than your mortal senses are able to apprehend. If you accept the fact that the split atom has revealed to you that all matter is energy and attempt to realize that the solid objects you see are actually composed mostly of space, why can you not envision the possibility that outer space also contains energy, and that structures similar to yours exist in a dimension you are unable to see?

Of course, spirits cannot see this wonderland either until they raise their thoughts to a point where it is revealed to them. None of the beauty can be perceived by those whose minds are bent only on what they already know and previously have experienced. Those earthbound souls who clutter up our space with their ignorance are only remaining close to earth because they will not lift their thoughts higher. We want them to accept what we tell them and come with us, but they are stuck where they are for various reasons: Either they are already what they think of as happy languishing in a less advanced state or they are miserable in a hellish condition of misapprehension they are unable to bring themselves to leave. Whichever way, they will do nothing about it. The time will eventually come when they will start to improve themselves, but the waste is tremendous until then.

In the meantime those who are progressing live in a beautiful world in the company of fascinating people who are all doing work that is challenging and stimulating to them. There also is a lot of playing. A sense of humor is very important, and having fun is a necessary part of our development. Although we are usually working during the day, we could spend our nights in gay carousal if we wished, but an enlightened spirit would seldom desire anything so frivolous. But we do have much jollity, for even our work at improving ourselves is frequently arranged in the form of entertainment.

We also have time for all the creative and constructive enterprises we were not able to work into our busy schedules on earth. Fortunately, we also have much greater clarity of mind and capacity for remembering and so our educational procedures are easier and more successful. Making ourselves more erudite, then, is not the problem it so often is for you. Concentrating is not so difficult either. We can place our attention on something to the exclusion of all else. Therefore, we can go ahead with all the academic and cultural improvements many of us always wished for but never had the time or opportunity to indulge in.

Much of every day may be spent acting as guardian angels, working for earth persons while at the same time attending to our own spiritual advancement. When the mortals we are working with go to sleep, we leave and then have the entire night for ourselves, although, of course, we are always on call if a need for us arises. If they awaken and begin to worry terribly or become ill or in some other way need our assistance, we go to them. But the rest of the night our attention may be centered on visits with friends, and on doing what we wish to do for pleasure and education.

Many of us will choose to go back to school for a time. If we did not complete our education, we will probably want to acquire the equivalent of college degrees. Available are courses under some of the greatest instructors who ever lived, as well as others who have gained the status of professors by their efforts since coming over here. Those who have mutual interests are attracted to each other; and so much of value is being discussed and explained everywhere that we find it difficult to decide which cluster of seekers around a teacher to join. We may enter any of these groups we wish. Those who are on their way upward are always welcome wherever they go. Snobbery does not exist among enlightened spirits. No one is rich while another is poor. There is no such thing as social position. All status is earned. No charge is made for anything and so each individual can afford the same as everyone else. If he does not have certain possessions, it is either because he does not want them or has not learned how to achieve them with his mind power.

Language is sometimes at first a barrier in the Etheric Plane. Advanced spirits have learned to communicate entirely by telepathy, expressing their ideas by visualization of images and symbols. They can thus talk with citizens of any country on earth, whether or not they had a common language. In addition, as they progress to higher planes, aware spirits are able to communicate telepathically with residents of any other planets in the universe.

But when you first enter the Etheric, you are untrained to use your thoughts in this manner. You are told how to employ telepathy, but it usually takes some time to assimilate this information and put it to use. You tend, therefore, to mingle with those you know or others from the areas of your world where your own language is spoken. Thus, if you wish to take advantage of an interchange of ideas and information with those of other countries, you may find it expedient to spend some time studying a foreign language or two if you had not learned other tongues on earth. You will discover real pleasure in becoming bilingual or trilingual.

Scientific inquiry is a major concern here, and you may wish to attend some classes or do some laboratory work on any of the research projects under way that fit within your areas of knowledge or usefulness or line of inquiry.

During your night's activities, if you have first attended a lecture and a language class and perhaps worked in a lab, you will probably now be ready for some cultural entertainment, and you will look for it according to your particular interests. The most magnificent music imaginable is here to be enjoyed. Yes, you hear it just as realistically as you do on earth, even though it is a matter of concentrating on it with your mind. Your senses are all much more alert and in perfect working order, and so music sounds much greater than it ever did to you before.

Everyone who ever had any musical talent has discovered as he progresses that it is his obligation to himself to learn as much as he can about music. It is not a matter of some kind of gatekeeper or disciplinarian standing at the entrance to the next sphere saying, "Thou shalt not pass until you have made the most of all your talents." No, it is that you, yourself, will know as you progress that you have not improved as much as possible and that there are some areas in which you have not yet achieved proper advancement. Those who have musical talents or interests, therefore, will now find the time to study, practice and participate in musical events. Students are learning violin, piano, sitar, and any other instruments they choose. Advanced pupils are holding recitals. Orchestras in all stages of maturity are performing concerts. Composers who had not accomplished as much with their talents as they now feel to be necessary are writing music of great beauty, and it is played by many of the students. You will be welcome into any recital or performance. If the program is of earth music it will probably be familiar to you. If it includes works by composers writing from their advanced spiritual understanding, you will hear music so superior to any you have ever heard before that your soul will be elevated to heights of glory as you listen.

Another night you may visit an art exhibit where paintings and sculpture by many newcomers are being shown, along with great masterpieces by progressed spirits. I must admit that certain of your modern absurdities are not on exhibit in our heavenly planes. We have so much that is wonderful that we do not allow ourselves to be distracted by the trivial. And, it must be remembered, we do not have to think of what will sell. We have only to express the best that is within us.

Do you like the theater? Many great productions are running. You may attend, or you may act in anything being arranged, if there is a role not already cast that you are capable of handling. If a show is not presently casting or has no place for you, you may start a production of your own and ask others to share the stage with you. It is amazing what fulfillment one can have in the theater when he does not have to wait for a terrestrial "angel" to back his play, or when a first-night critic cannot blackball it out of existence. You will be able to be either your own producer, manager, director, or star, and can run the performance as long as it is of value to you to do so. Of course, you would not intrude yourself upon professionals until you are ready, but your talent in acting may soon improve until you find yourself a hit in every sense of the word.

After spending a certain amount of time on your cultural improvement and development of your talents, you will perhaps wish then to play with your hobbies or games. Do you like to dance?

There are ballet classes for beginners as well as the more advanced, and great dancing artists are teaching those especially talented; but there are also many who are dancing merely for pleasure. There are parties for those who wish to cavort for fun without bothering to train themselves in any new routines, just continuing the steps popular in their day on earth. Folk dancing of all countries goes on whenever groups from the same region meet. Yes, I have even seen jitterbugging here. This newest twisting and jiggling about and watusiing or bugalooing or whatever it is your young people are doing now does not seem to have come over here yet, probably because so few of that age have died.

Perhaps you enjoyed cards. I have seen many poker games in heaven. And if you can gamble without letting it disturb your equilibrium, you are perfectly free to wager as much as you desire. After all, it is only money or matchsticks or pins, and there is plenty more where that came from. You may be surprised to learn that outwitting your opponents at games of skill is just as exciting even when there are no really crucial stakes.

Bridge enthusiasts, too, quite frequently manage to take time out for a game. It is not considered good form for beginners to attempt to play with those who are in Masters' competition, but then enlightened beginners would know better than to ask. You will find plenty of eager participants in a game at your own level. I have never heard that the problem of finding a fourth for bridge is at all prevalent here. No one, you see, has to hunt for a baby-sitter, drive through traffic halfway across town, or remain home because of illness. And no one refrains from going out at night for fear of being mugged.

There are many other pleasures in spirit realms that might surprise you. I have even seen some who have died in recent years sitting in front of television sets carefully watching your earthly soap operas. This cannot be considered fun, surely! But they do seem to relish it.

COMMENTARY:
I told James if I couldn't watch M*A*S*H in heaven, I'd stick around here a few more years until the series has run its course. He said that would probably be a good idea anyway.

Those who never missed a baseball game of their favorite teams are still attending with the human crowds at the ballparks. Many spirits continue to root for their college football teams or yell and scream for their basketball or hockey favorites. Horse racing also has its devoted adherents.

In case some moralist assumes from this that I am suggesting that heaven is "wide open," I believe I have shown that a gradual transition from earthly pleasures to delights of a more meaningful nature is invariably successfully accomplished, and that carefree pleasure is an attribute to be encouraged. With all this, then, we find that life is never dull after progression has begun. Advancement makes for enlightenment, and enlightenment makes for enjoyment.

Susy tells me here that I have made heaven sound so attractive that people will be committing suicide in order to get here faster. This, of course, is completely ill advised. Killing yourself, for any reason, is as bad as killing another. Whatever you have not learned on earth because of the deliberately shortened life experience must be made up in the Etheric plane in ways so much more difficult that, believe me, it is better to stay where you are and stick it out, no matter what terrible situation you may find yourself facing or how many joys you anticipate in the future. Remember that however unpleasant your life is and however promising the next life may appear to you, enduring the situation you are in to the best of your abilities makes for much faster and easier progression later. Suicide is such an appalling act that I will speak of it at length later.

By the time you have begun your progression, you will be spending less and less time in pursuits of an earthly nature, but those you will continue to enjoy will be even more fulfilling. Forever and always you will take pleasure in music, and heavenly music is so much more heavenly than any you have previously experienced that you will be continually delighted. It is true that color is involved with everything here, much more so than on earth. Color and music form a harmonious whole so amazing that you will be eternally enthralled by it.

Color here is not just an attribute of matter; it is part of our very existence. Color is an actual separate reality, a part of us, part of our lives, an element of our very existence. Music is the same. We don't just listen to music, we experience it. It is within us, surrounding us, encompassing us.

There are other qualities that make our lives more stimulating and more joyous than you could possibly believe. Love is not just a word to us; it is not just a feeling or an emotion. It interpenetrates us all, overwhelming us. Our attunement to it is our foremost step upward. More and more our existence is intermingled with the all-pervading love of the universe, of which human love is only a small part. And yet human love, too, is much more successful and much more thrilling when truly enjoyed here. Those who have shared a great love on earth will continue to enjoy it after their deaths, and often those who have not had a truly good emotional experience will find one after coming here. Yet human love, or any other love in the Etheric plane, can give us only the barest idea of the kind of overwhelming love and bliss we will experience constantly when the time comes that we finally learn to achieve our true potential, absorbing and sharing the illimitable love of Ultimate Perfection.

IX
STARTING UPWARD

It may surprise you, but you will not immediately soar up and out of the Etheric plane just because you were a good Christian or Buddhist or Muslim, or even because you went in for philosophical studies or humanitarian activities. You will certainly be way in advance of those who had no such head start, but you may still have much improving to do on many other aspects of your personality and character. And you will have to work your way up like anyone else.

The process of Evolutionary Soul Progression cannot permit anyone who is less than a paragon to reach Ultimate Perfection, and so no matter how high a state you are in when you die, you still have much more to accomplish. And most of that general learning development is done before you leave the Etheric. The refining and perfecting is achieved in higher planes.

Even one who lived a life dedicated to helping others has to continue to exert himself in order to progress. This is because each individual must become perfected in all areas of his character, not just certain ones. I will illustrate this with the story of a man to whom we will give the name Harry Wright.

Harry had lived for love of his fellow men. He went into the profession of caseworker for the public welfare program just because he thought he could do the most good there. He was always on call to run errands for his friends and his clients, to lend them money, to go to court for them if necessary. It was never possible to find Harry unwilling to do anyone a favor. He was always with someone who was in need, giving his time and attention when it was required.

When Harry died, he naturally attracted the immediate attention of spirits of a very high type. He rejoiced when he learned the things he must do for his soul's harmony, especially glad that he could become a guardian angel. Now he would be able to help many more people. He soon learned to project his thoughts so insistently that many who had known him before his death felt his presence from beyond. He loved them and aided them so much that their lives were even smoother because he had passed on and was able to give so much more of himself to them.

Harry could easily have become so involved in his program of helpfulness, just as he had on earth, that he did nothing else. But if you think because he was so sympathetic that he was ready to go to the heights, you are wrong. Harry had never paid enough attention to himself, and now he must learn to do that. He had not developed many other areas of his personality and character. He had never even had much fun in life, and now he had a lot of merriment to catch up on. He had seldom played games and enjoyed lighthearted pleasures, but they, too, are essential to his overall completion. One never sees a truly advanced spirit who does not have a smile and a twinkling eye. And so Harry had to go in for sports and games of all kinds, join clubs, and spend a certain portion of his life just plain having a good time. He did not find this at all hard to accept, when he learned the reason for it and stopped feeling guilty whenever he took time out from helping others to enjoy himself.

Harry also learned that he had been born with the capabilities of becoming a splendid sculptor. He had never done a thing about it on earth, although he had loved art and wished he could attempt it; he had not even realized that he had more than average talent in that direction. Now he came to understand his true potentialities and was faced with the fact that he must perfect them all. He became aware that until he had advanced in creativity, among other things, he could not leave the Etheric. He must apply himself to his efforts to learn sculpture, and he must continue to do so until he attained facility in the art. Of course, he took great pleasure in it, hardly realizing he was doing it in order to achieve a new dimension to his character and personality.

At this point Susy asks for a clearer explanation of how he would go about sculpturing in the Astral plane. He has first to think up a supply of clay and the wood for his armatures and the tools he will need. Then physically, with his hands, as he would have done on earth, he builds the armature and puts the clay on it and starts to mold it into shape.

Harry Wright had been so involved with helping others that he had never acquired any advanced college degrees. Therefore, he had a lot of actual classes and lectures, seminars and workshops to attend. But he enjoyed every minute. I don't want you to think that he did not achieve his advancement quickly and happily, because he did. He had a definite head start in the things most people take the longest to learn—to love and work for others. But my point is that this alone did not make him anywhere near perfect.

For those who are, like Harry Wright, so advanced spiritually when they come over here that they know the importance of making every effort to love their fellow men and keep their thoughts at a constructive level, progress starts immediately. Because we have no element of time to obstruct us, there is no problem about getting everything done we undertake to do. After all, we have all eternity! So if it seems to you that Harry has taken on an awfully big project of self-improvement, he has. But he has no feeling of pressure about accomplishing it.

It is to be hoped that all you good readers will arrive in our dimension as Harry did, full of loving kindness. Then every aspect of the work you undertake will be interesting from the beginning. Nothing will seem dull or routine for you, for whatever you are doing can always be made pleasurable. Life after one has begun his progression becomes unbelievably happy at all times.

COMMENTARY:

I do not want the reader ever to think I am being flippant about any aspect of the James material. I take it all very seriously, quote it frequently, and am completely captured by the ideas presented. But on occasion I tend to talk to my invisible friend as if he were a father or an uncle and tell him what I think. And sometimes I tell him he is just too repetitious. He may then allow me to remove some of the duplications that bother me; but in many instances he maintains that this is deliberate so that his message will be more effective. He is no doubt right. In fact, he has often been proved right.

When I lived in Miami, I was interviewed occasionally by Bill Smith on radio station WKAT's Talk of Miami program, and he became quite interested in hearing about James' communications as they were received. When the manuscript was completed, Bill read it. He agreed with me at first about the repetitiveness, feeling that some of it—which I have since cut out—was almost tedious in a few spots because of the redundancy. And yet several months later Bill remarked that he found himself remembering vast amounts of information that had been quite new to him before he read the manuscript. He said he was convinced that James' tendency to recapitulation was the reason it had stuck with him.

In an unpublished Stewart Edward White manuscript, an entity known as Gaelic says: "You think that life tells you many things; and it is telling you over and over a few; presenting them tirelessly in multiform, until at last the one appropriate rendition brings illumination. The multiplicity of Nature's devices are a means of telling you the same thing over and over again, in different forms, until the apt phrase makes you understand."

In this book, for "Nature" read "James."

But how does it fare with someone who does not come over in an already enlightened state? He may cling to his old condition for a great while, but eventually he will start to work attempting to improve himself. When he does, he is told immediately how to begin thinking positively and loving others at all times. He is given various techniques for attempting this and assured that he will have help all the way. Not for a moment is he left alone, unless he prefers to be. He is assisted in a manner very similar to that used by Alcoholics Anonymous. Those who have had to learn self-improvement in the hardest way possible because they died in completely degraded states now spend their time aiding their fellows who have similar problems. As, with their help, he begins to think in terms of making something of himself, he may first be taken to a ballgame or to some kind of amusement that he will enjoy in order to reveal to him that this is possible. Then he is shown around to all the things his perception is now becoming capable of letting him see, so that he can realize what a potentially beautiful world he is really in. He is also given the opportunity to attend some lectures that will inspire him to go on with his efforts. After a time he will discuss with his mentors what kind of work would be most suitable for him to start with. Realizing that by aiding others he will also be doing the most to help himself, he will probably first undertake a program of that nature.

It may be that the individual undergoing spiritual rebirth becomes particularly interested in someone who is serving in the armed forces. Although he may have been so degraded when he died that he cared for no one, now he decides to make it his business to work among the large groups that are often called brotherhoods—spirits who act as greeters of all who are killed in wars. If there is no war involving his country going on at the time, he can give the same kind of attention to those who die in disasters or accidents. Special effort is made to welcome every one of these persons so that they will not arrive suddenly into a new phase of life without knowing what to expect. Many who die in battle will awaken in the warm embrace of relatives who have preceded them in death. But those who have no family to watch out for them while they are involved in war efforts are very grateful for the receiving line of gracious, if unknown, spirits who make it their business to greet and carefully indoctrinate newcomers.

After seeing the pitiful mental condition in which some soldiers arrive in our sphere—full of hatred for the enemy who killed them or the government that sent them to war in the first place, grief-stricken because they have left a sweetheart or a family who are longing for them, or anguished at a life so summarily cut short in youth—the spirit helpers attempt to give all the consolation possible. They try to show these young men they have not reached the end of life, but are only starting on an exciting new phase of it. The advancing spirit working in the brotherhood is now in the position his own greeters were in shortly before. He is learning and growing as he instructs others.

When a spirit, frequently a childless woman, is deciding what one of her first projects will be, she may think of something she has always really wanted to do—raise children. She can not now produce any of her own in the Etheric . . . no. Only God can provide the consciousness that is to become human; so no matter how hard one tries to envision a baby for herself, it would be a fruitless endeavor. However, someone has to raise the many babies who die and will grow to manhood or womanhood in the Astral plane. Remember that the spirit body is the pattern, not just a duplicate of the physical body. Naturally the pattern can continue to grow without the physical organism to accompany it. So it is not hard to understand that a child can attain adulthood in the spirit world. When a helper chooses to raise one, she can lavish on him all the affection and attention she would have given a child of her own, and he will grow up happily fulfilled. Of course, other attendant spirits will keep careful watch on all the helpers do and often give them advice.

Other areas in which a great deal of assistance is needed and a fantastic number of workers are involved are the attempts to instruct potential earthbound entities. Many who are killed suddenly, before they have the spiritual awareness to understand their situation, those who succumb in charity hospitals, jails or any other sordid conditions, and criminals, particularly, are always received as friends. If they are willing to listen and pay attention, they may never become earthbound at all but may start their progress at once. If they do not, those with low character may cling to their old ways interminably before they finally decide to listen.

You think you have ecology problems! You certainly do. But consider ours. The atmosphere in and around and over many large cities contains an invisible crush of earthbound entities who are just not willing to listen to the many spirit helpers available to answer questions. We must start them moving, but it is a terrible chore for us to do so. That is why we are so eager to get the word to you on earth so that so many won't keep coming over here to us in such a low state.

It is most helpful if the newly progressing spirit will spend some time on this rescue work, and he will probably feel a responsibility to do so. It is so disheartening, however, that he may go on to other jobs from time to time, only coming back to the earthbound after what might be called rest periods.

The most common form of development is the spirit guardian or guardian angel. Many who die are still extremely interested in the welfare of a spouse, child or parents who remain on earth. If a spirit decides to work in behalf of someone he loves, he may have many problems to cope with vicariously as he stays close and becomes involved in this person's life. Although sometimes he may get through to him or her, he again may find that none of his helpful advice is taken and his presence is always ignored. This is not surprising because he is not seen, and his talk falls on deaf ears unless the recipient is psychic or is attempting to "tune in" to make contact with him. So here I must give a word of suggestion to the living:

It is quite necessary that those of you who have lost someone realize that he is most likely still around you as closely as before, even though now in an invisible and inaudible form. This may seem an imposition to some who have longed to be free of encumbering responsibilities. Others who loved deeply and were much loved in return may feel that it is the kindness of Fate that allows the beloved to remain with them. But no matter what your attitude, the fact remains—if we have any interest in you at all, we do not leave you when we die. We are even closer than before, for now we know exactly what you are thinking at all times whenever we care to pay attention. (Sensitivity among the higher type citizen of the spirit world will of course cause him to refrain from eavesdropping at intimate or especially private moments in your life.)

As you can see, there is much work to be done from our side, work that is of service to others, but that also gives the spirit an opportunity to develop other areas of growth to which he might not otherwise have been exposed. In giving himself for the assistance of those who need him, he is also working for his own development, and as he lives each day for others, he will soon realize that he has to think very little about his own soul's progress. He is improving himself without consciously trying.

X

THE GOLDEN CHAIN

THERE IS WHAT might be likened to a great golden chain of love and understanding linking up each individual consciousness with all others and with Divine Consciousness. Those on the higher planes are aware of this, while most of you on earth and in the lower spheres of the spirit world are completely oblivious to it. All advanced entities are eager to impart their knowledge and the benefit of their experience to others for use in their own spiritual evolution. We who receive their enlightenment and love in turn transmit it to those who have acquired sufficient growth of soul to be receptive.

One link of the golden chain is the guardian angel of whom I have spoken. This is just a colloquial term used by us to refer to those who, as a means of self-improvement as well as helpfulness, give their time to assisting specific individuals on earth. These may be persons they love, those with certain affinities, such as mutual interests, or those who need to learn certain lessons that the guardian angel also needs to learn. There is a very definite distinction between a guardian angel, who is a newly developing spirit and an actual "angel," who is a spirit advanced to the heights.

When our period of self-evaluation begins after our deaths, and we realize that we are lacking in certain areas of understanding and experience, we will begin to rectify it; and this is done in part with the help of those more progressed than we are. As they assist us, we in turn expend our efforts on those below us in the evolutionary scale—the newcomers in the spirit world who are of low advancement and those on earth to whom we are guardian angels. Thus, we, too, are very definite links in the golden chain of love and understanding.

Those more advanced than we are give us advice about the steps we should take to develop character traits we do not have. We are told that all the conditions necessary for learning are available to us right here in the Etheric. It is not necessary for anyone to go back on earth and live another life in order to acquire the experiences he has missed. We can learn lessons instead by consciously applying our attention to them in the spirit world. We will then usually discover that we can acquire a thorough understanding of our own personality problems by staying with an earth person who needs to gain knowledge in similar areas. So we will become his guardian angel for a while and give him all the support we are able. Of course, a guardian angel is always careful not to try to make decisions for his wards; but if he can alleviate some of their problems or guide them into taking wiser steps, they will benefit from his company. He, too, will learn as he observes the learning processes in another. It is proverbial that the teacher gains more than the pupils do. Even an invisible teacher may do that.

It is by our own desire that we become guardian angels. No one forces us to do it. We actually intend to help ourselves as we help you; so do not ever feel that you are holding us against our will and keeping us from progressing by being with you. You aid us by being object lessons for us. When we see the involvements you get yourselves into, we also understand how they could have been avoided, and we learn from this as well.

Most people do not know they have guardian angels, and so it is possible that you have been unaware of the existence of yours, if you have one. Actually his or her identity is not important, although if there is someone who has a legitimate interest in you who has passed over, you can reasonably expect him to be the one. Even if you have no idea who he could be, however, just conclude that you very likely have a guardian angel and try to let him give you assistance. You are not at all apt to be wrong. And especially if you express a desire for one, you certainly will have the golden chain extended to you, if you do not already have it.

Taking it for granted that your guardian angel is there, try to be receptive to him. After you say your prayers at night or while you meditate, say to him, "Dear guardian angel, whoever you are, thank you for being with me. I'll accept any help you can give me." And then really make an effort to do just that.

Those of you who are open-minded about this idea can benefit; if you are closed to it, you will never allow any possible assistance to penetrate your armor. Those whose minds are shut tight against anything of a spiritual nature usually remain in such a negative attitude that they are never aware of any invisible helping hands that might be of value to them. It is quite possible for very beautiful souls to be materialists. I do not mean to imply that if you do not believe in the possibility of life after death, you may not be a splendid individual; you might very well be.

The idea that you could possibly be receiving assistance from some unseen entity might even be repulsive to you, for you like to think of yourself as the captain of your ship, the master of your soul. However, a spirit guide operating constructively in your behalf will take nothing away from your own development, and could add immeasurably to it. Many who reject this concept may eventually find that their lives do not reveal all the positive values they had hoped. When illness, poverty or other large problems intervene—most particularly the death of someone greatly beloved—sometimes such a materialist begins to reach for a truer understanding of life. Then, if he turns to God, he opens his defenses so that his guardian angel can get through to him and give assistance. Yet when he finds his life becoming more tolerable again, he will probably still be reluctant to admit that "spooks" had anything to do with it.

Now let me tell you how a spirit who is beginning his progression and decides he can best help himself by helping others goes about it. When an enlightened man dies, his first exciting discovery, after his reunion with his loved ones, is that all his memories are intact and available to him. If he wishes to remember any moment of his life, it is there in all detail. For a while he may have fun recalling persons and places he has not thought of in years. He soon becomes aware that this can cause him real anguish, however, as he allows himself to relive some of his most traumatic experiences. So he stops the self-torture. When he begins his progression, it will be necessary for him to make a systematic survey of his life, to go into all his memories carefully to learn where he made mistakes and to recall all the occasions when he did less than his best. Many unhappy events will have to be reviewed in detail so that he can learn what to do to make amends. He is now in a position to see the reasons for many of the errors he made, even those early in life. Some of them can be rectified by thinking them through from a constructive point of view and understanding all the situations involved. Others may have been so unfortunate that more will have to be done in order to correct them. Yet each incident of his life will have to be gone over with the object of making amends for anything that requires it. In many cases he may, even at this late date, be able to alter the situation for the better by his proper thinking and corrective mental application.

To pay a debt he cannot pay in any other way he may decide to become a guardian angel for someone whom he may have hurt exceedingly. An example is a man who deceived a woman into thinking he was going to marry her. He then left her heartbroken. After his death he wants to do something to make up to her for this. He certainly is not able to marry her then, nor would either of them wish it; but he must do something to help her. It may be that she has already forgiven him, has realized that he would not have made her a good husband, and perhaps has married someone else and had a relatively happy life with him. The fact remains that this man treated this woman shabbily at one time in her life, and he now wants to make it up to her, even though she may have no idea he is now working in her behalf. If she doesn't personally need much assistance at the time, perhaps he will be a guardian angel to her daughter for a while, in order to keep her from being victimized in a similar way. It is not now considered such bad taste as it was in my day to make love to a woman and not marry her. Still, many have broken hearts because they have been treated cavalierly, so you will surely allow me to hypothesize a man who now has regrets for such an act, even if you think of him as old-fashioned. When the daughter is growing up, therefore, this spirit will be with her to give her mental guidance whenever possible. She may begin to wonder why it is that she has intuitive feelings about her suitors, somehow instinctively knowing whom she can trust and whom she cannot. She may have what she begins to think of as a sixth sense about what is going to occur with them.

So by helping her daughter this man who jilted the woman may compensate her without in any way letting her know. It really does not matter whether or not she knows; although if she did, it would give her a warmer feeling about an incident that once hurt her deeply. And his deed of recompense has been of value to him as he has watched the girl and has seen her problems of various sorts with men. It clarifies for him how his own thinking had been in error when he was a youth.

As an example of how you go about remaking yourself, let us suppose that in reviewing your life you discover that you had a great many prejudices of a very deep-seated nature. You may have taken adequate care of your family and died thinking that in general you were a relatively decent sort of chap. Proper reconnaissance of your life now, however, reveals that there was one entire area in which you had a complete blank spot: You had racial prejudice. Therefore, no matter how tolerant you believed yourself to have been in other areas, you actually have a tremendous amount to learn. When it was impossible for you to think of a Negro as anything but an inferior person, you yourself are inferior. Or if you, as a black man, blamed all your white brothers for the injustices perpetrated by specific individuals, you were equally guilty of racial prejudice. You actually hated mankind, loved only those who were like yourself, and so truly loved no man.

Now that you have faced the fact that you went through life with a distorted image of the truth, you will have to decide how to correct it. You will discuss it with those of your associates who are more advanced than you; you go to a teacher and listen to some of his lectures on this problem and how to cope with it. You will be told that until you can feel equally at home with anyone who is black or white or yellow or red or any beautiful tint in between, you will not have learned brotherly love.

If you were a white man with this problem of learning compassion, you will probably now decide that the best form of growth for you is to go to live in the terrestrial home of an underprivileged Negro. This will not be easy for you at first, when, without understanding the deprivations of poverty, you may have constant revulsion from what you consider a lowly way of life. Much of your effort in the beginning will have to be spent just in keeping yourself from leaving your appointed task. But after a while you will find yourself becoming absorbed in the daily lives of the family with whom you are making your home.

From your vantage point of invisibility, you will be able to observe everything that happens in this family's life, and you will be aware of what each member is thinking. Soon you will begin to know what it means to be a black man in a predominantly white civilization. Then you will become sympathetic and will want to do all you can for these people. How will you accomplish it? Your thoughts are all you have to work with, and so anything you attempt will be difficult for you, but perseverance will win.

Let us say, for instance, that you learn by secretly visiting around in the town that a white racist extremist is putting a bomb under the house of the black family with whom you live. What will you do? Warn them, you naturally think. But how? Once in a great while a spirit finds conditions such that he is able to make himself seen or heard. Certainly if this family saw a ghost they would run out of the house quickly enough. Even if they heard an audible warning from you they would very likely heed it. But making a physical manifestation from the spirit world takes a great deal of effort, unless the psychokinetic forces from earth are exactly right. If you haven't the power available to make yourself appear in a ghostly form or cause yourself to be heard, perhaps you can arouse in the most psychic member of the family a vision or dream that will give him the warning. If none of these measures is effective, you will attempt to alert someone to the danger they are in. You might find one receptive enough that you can get through to him; he will then think he has a hunch to look under the porch, where he finds the bomb before it is set to go off, or he warns the others to vacate the house in time to escape the explosion.

However, in the short time you have, you may get nowhere. On such a pressing occasion, you may repeat your admonitions endlessly, giving them all the force and thought power within you, without achieving results. The only thing to do then is to stick your fingers in your ears and wait for the blast, realizing that, if nothing else, the way members of the family accept the tragedy will give them an opportunity to build character. I am quite sure that by the time the bomb has exploded and you are trying somehow to aid the bleeding children, your aversion to black men will have changed altogether.

You will probably then have to work on your emotions to keep from blindly hating the whites who have perpetrated this crime.

It is seldom that you are likely to come up against a situation quite as dramatic as a bombing; but other events will be nearly as impressive to you. If you have stayed with this family any length of time, you will undoubtedly have become fond of the children. It is not possible to look into the mind of a child and not learn to love him. Now, what if you should begin to realize that the ten-year-old boy of the family is exposed to the danger of becoming a juvenile delinquent? You would certainly make every possible effort to guide him in a different direction—and your thoughts are practically your only contact with him, remember. You will beam him constructive ideas constantly, encouraging him to stay in school and study his lessons and refuse to try drugs. You may be able to guide his thinking toward going to Sunday school and associating with playmates who are less inclined to lead him astray. But you will undoubtedly tend to become desperate about the boy on occasion—as hopeless as the mother and father who are aware of the importance of his acquiring a sense of values that will not be corrupted yet do not know how to encourage and protect him adequately.

It will not be easy to aid this family with only your thoughts; but as you come to understand the problems of these people, you will be learning to love your fellow men. By the time you have lived a lifetime with them, watching the boy grow to manhood—perhaps becoming a good citizen largely because of the influence of your positive thoughts for him—you will have a genuine knowledge of what it means to walk in the shoes of a black man. Will it then be possible for you to feel superior to any race? How can a man reject another by the color of his skin when he knows deeply all the problems that beset the heart of one of such pigmentation?

Now, perhaps in evaluating your life you discover that you were especially prejudiced against those who had different habits from yours, particularly if they had them to excess. It is necessary for you to overcome your intolerance, even of evildoers. In other words, you have every reason to hate the crime but not the criminal. Intolerance is bigotry. A bigot may declare his dislike of a vice, but he will seldom make any effort to assist those who have such weaknesses, because he thinks himself superior to them. Perhaps whenever you encountered a drunkard during your lifetime, you scorned him instead of pitying him. Now you must learn to love him! How will you do it? You will go and live with an alcoholic and attempt to help him by being a guardian angel to him.

Perhaps there was such an afflicted person in your acquaintance. Instead of realizing that he was sick, you reviled and scorned him and spoke of him disparagingly to his neighbors and friends. Now, after your self-evaluation, you realize that you must learn to have compassion for such a man as this, to the point of understanding him and his problems; and so you choose to assist him as part of your personal campaign for self-improvement.

In this man's home, reading his mind, you begin to understand the terrible humiliation he undergoes each time he comes out of one of his drinking episodes. You observe what an intolerable hardship it is on him to realize what he has done to his family and to know that he cannot make amends for it. You hear the impossible arguments he has within himself before he succumbs once again to his desire for drink. And you recognize his physical lack of the proper bodily components that causes his illness in the first place. Can you now judge him?

When you also become aware that around this man with the alcohol problem, there are a number of earthbound entities who incite him to drink and make his resistance ineffective, you will be even more eager to help him rid himself of his difficulties. Talking to those spirits who hang around him, attempting to convince them that their existence will always be sordid if they stay so close to earth's unhappiest people, you will occasionally be able to give them new ideas, which may cause them to start their progression and leave the poor alcoholic. If you can do this for him, your time with him will have been well spent for everyone concerned. As for your own reaction—you will now understand fully the problems of a drinker, and you will have grown a great deal in wisdom.

A few more efforts of this sort on your part will turn you into a truly compassionate spirit, and then you can work on other aspects of your character in which you recognize weaknesses. You may wish to go on being a guardian angel for a while as you do so, and most especially you will spend a lot of time with someone you love who is still on earth. You have probably visited him or her frequently while you have been working with these other people, and you may have already assisted him in many ways by your proper thinking about his problems.

It may sound difficult for you to have to give assistance to others in order to improve yourself. It is; but all self-improvement is difficult, whether living the problems presented you in your own earth life, or sharing those of others after your death. But always remember, once you have grasped hold of the golden chain of love and understanding, and put your feet on the ladder of upward progression, nothing can stop you. You will be so entranced with the adventures you are having, and so interested to see the results, that you will greet happily each new opportunity that presents itself to grow through being of service to others.

XI

THE SAD, SAD STATE OF THE EARTHBOUND

The rate of your initial advancement after death depends at first on your progress on earth. It is not a matter of reward in the hereafter for good behavior or punishment for bad. It is a matter of success or failure as a person. If you have lived a life of love and service, you will feel a sense of joyous participation in the universal warmth almost immediately, and you will go forward quickly and happily.

But if you have existed for self alone, considering your pleasures and comforts more important than anything else, living only for the sensations you could cram into each moment, your forward movement after death will start only after a long period of delay, when you finally learn the importance of attaining harmony with Universal Good. Until then you will be an earthbound spirit, and you will truly live in a hell of your own making.

Man is given free will and the ability to choose his own path; however, many elect to gratify their physical senses and carnal desires so entirely that their lives are either criminal, totally selfish, debauched, corrupt, depraved or dissolute, and their paths are downward. This is unfortunate because it is much easier to have gained wisdom on earth than to have to reverse a trend after death and undo all the harm you have done to yourself and others before you can ever achieve growth.

The griefs and tribulations of an ordinary lifetime cause much unhappiness; but when you think about it, you will realize that it is through them that you have learned the most. How much has your temperament actually improved during the placid, uneventful periods of your life? It is the pressures you strive against that build character. Those who have only become embittered about their lot have gained little from experience, and they will have a miserable existence after death until they face up to the truth.

Whatever the cause of his low state—bad ancestry, poor environment, poverty, too much wealth, not enough mother love, too much "smother" love, nutritional deficiencies, bad companions, bad habits—a thief or murderer or unregenerate spirit has no sense of values. Besides those who think themselves so degraded that nothing can be done for them, and those who believe themselves always right no matter what wicked things they do, there are others who are earthbound just because they are satisfied with their status quo, no matter how low it is. They have no incentive to improve.

We spirit missionaries try hard to love these earthbound delinquents, but they make it difficult for us. When we begin our efforts to save them, we knock on mental doors that are resolutely closed to our importuning. Existence is sordid and dark for these poor individuals—nothing is beautiful to the spiritually ugly—and they may wander for eons of time in a miasma of negativity. Through all this they will cling to their former customs, causing untold harm to those on earth who are under their influence or whom they hated. Yes, their thoughts can be damaging, bringing all kinds of ill fortune to those who do not know how to protect themselves from them.

Many who are in no way criminal or profligate are still held to earth for one reason or another. It is even possible for one whose motives are entirely well-intentioned to be earthbound. A mother, for instance, who has been so possessive of her family that life holds nothing else for her may continue her concentration on them in a negative manner.

Rita Sanchez was such a mother. She lived only for her children, giving up everything for them, denying herself many pleasures in their behalf. Naturally she was thought of as a good mother, but she was a tenacious one instead. She did nothing for self-improvement because all her time was given to coddling her offspring. Later she devoted herself to her grandchildren, baby-sitting, moving in when necessary to help one who was sick, taking over the housekeeping and child care willingly . . . much too willingly, some of her daughters-in-law thought. Rita seemed to be a kindly person, but she was completely taken up with what was hers. Her affection was not really given except to those who belonged to her. All her attention through her life was on her "own" with such a selfish love it was hardly love at all.

When Rita Sanchez died, she had much to learn. She did nothing about it, however, her thoughts still centered on those she had left behind. No family discussion took place without her there, putting in her suggestions and doing all she could to run things as she had in the past. The fact that she was now unseen and unheard did not keep her from actively participating. Such was her concentration that if she particularly wanted something done, it frequently was done because of her mental efforts. When she thought one son should leave a wife she did not feel was good enough for him, she constantly insinuated critical thoughts into his mind. Soon he was unable to see any merit in his spouse, and he separated from her. Mother gloated; yet her son would never have believed it if he had been told she was influencing him from the grave.

Rita was hindering her children in many ways. And until all the members of the family were in the spirit world, she did nothing about her own progression. When they had come over and she had greeted them one by one, she began her bossing all over again. If they listened to her petty ideas, sometimes they were not as quick to start the upward path as they might otherwise have been. So Rita was a detriment to those she loved, and she was even more so to herself. Eventually, of course, when her family has all gone ahead of her, she will start taking the steps necessary to catch up. Fortunately, by the time she has perfected herself, she will realize that she does not have to overtake or influence anyone who does not want her with him. She will have learned to be an individual, complete and happy and entirely successful in herself.

Money or property can sometimes make a person unwilling to give up earthly contacts and unable to accept his new conditions. It is not easy to leave possessions you have grown to love more than you love wisdom or strength of mind. And so you may cling to them. When you are told that it is possible to make replicas of your beloved possessions for yourself, it may be the impetus to get you started toward learning to use your thoughts properly. You could for a time become involved in producing objects to the exclusion of all else, basking in the pleasure of owning them once again; but mastering any technique is progressing, and soon you will develop to the point where belongings mean little to you and you become happily aware of the beauties of nature and the loving friendliness of others.

Those who are addicted to habitual drinking or dope will have difficulty learning to live without them. At first they do not even try. They attempt vicariously to continue to enjoy their vices by sharing those of earth addicts. An earthbound alcoholic will remain with a hard drinker, inciting him to further imbibing. If he took heroin on earth, he still thinks of himself as a "user," and he will stay with addicts and urge them on to additional excesses.

Mortals with a drug habit could rid themselves of it much more quickly if they were aware that part of the problem of their addiction is the influence of spirits. Addiction, as doctors know, does not have to be permanent, and yet most of those who "kick the habit" come right back to it. It has indeed a great deal to do with their emotional insecurity and their living conditions, companions and customs; but it has a great deal more to do with the fact that earthbound spirits will not let them alone and continually urge them to resume their vices.

Unless you of degraded habits learn to beware of the dangers of influence from the earthbound, you will allow them to sway you. Then, if you are weak-willed and negative in your own personality, you may be led into crime, vice, or worse—suicide. Many have committed crimes or have taken their own lives because a voice, or even a mere strong impulse, continually pressured them. It might, for instance say, "Take a drink. You need a drink. You must have a drink," until they can no longer resist.

Of course, if in that state you go to a psychiatrist, he will treat you for psychosis. Many in institutions now are there because they hear voices or have strong compulsions to do things they do not really want to do, as if someone else were running their lives for them. No matter how ingenuous this concept sounds, if doctors would only realize that most of these persons are, in fact, being talked to by spirits, they could be cured.

COMMENTARY:
I once knew an attractive blonde who was an alcoholic. She fre-

quently used to feel the urge to take a drink, not as if it came from her own mind, but as if it were someone else talking to her. She knew that she was a person with psychic abilities, and she believed in the possibility of spirit communication. She nonetheless feared that her drinking problem was psychological. Events, however, seemed to indicate that she was instead obsessed by some earthbound entity. Even when not urging her to drink, he began to talk to her in her mind, telling her he loved her and wanted her with him. He said he would make her kill herself so that she would come over to his sphere. As she drove along in her car she would suddenly hear the words, plainly spoken in her mind, "Drive into that tree" or "Hit that telephone pole." This young woman fought this phenomenon for years, quite naturally suspecting that she had become insane yet fearing to approach a doctor with her problem because he might put her away.

She used to tell me about going to Alcoholics Anonymous meetings and sharing her experiences with some of the others who had similar compelling voices in their minds. By attending sessions regularly, she thought she had her problem licked. Then one night she took a pep pill. Somewhat high on that, she decided to have a drink . . . but she insists she took only one. Anyway, whatever . . . on her way home she had to turn her car wheels abruptly to dodge a careless pedestrian crossing the street. As she did so her invisible persuader demanded that she run into a telephone pole and she did, damaging her car frightfully and herself somewhat. In doing this she somehow managed to dislodge her tormentor, because she was not bothered by him for a long time afterward. Neither did she have the desire to take a drink when she knew she did not really want one; and so for a while she was able to maintain successful balance on the water wagon.

Unfortunately, she met a man at AA with whom she fell in love. When they began to have little quarrels and problems in their relationship, they both reverted to drink; the last I heard of my blond friend, she had all her unwanted spirit attentions again.

A good medium is of great help in discouraging earthbound entities from causing trouble. Mediums are often able to speak to these intruders and wake them to the truth of their situation; so no mental institution should be without the services of one for consultation.

Because of the importance of this knowledge to the world, sensitives, psychics and mediums should be primarily known as channels for messages that will reveal continued existence after death, although today not too many of them are developing their talents in this direction. They are finding that straight clairvoyance, healing or "past life" readings take much less training and preparation and are much more remunerative. Yet their ability to aid earthbound spirits is the most important talent they possess. It is possible for a psychic to allow a poor soul who needs enlightenment about the truth of his dismal condition to speak through him. A spirit's interest must first be caught so that he will listen when accurate information is given him. When this is done, he will then pay attention to the missionaries in his plane and begin his progression. This is why some Spiritualist churches have rescue circles in which the medium goes into a trance and low entities are allowed to speak through him. When they converse with the members of the circle and are told the truth about their condition, they will listen. They have known all along that something was wrong with them but have not realized what it was. When told the truth in such a way that they will pay attention, they are usually glad to accept it.

It might seem odd to you, but the unenlightened will listen to you better than they will listen to those in their own realm. This is because their attention is so centered on the earth that they can see and hear you more readily than they can those of us on their own side of life. If you once reach their ears with the truth, then they are more likely to hear us when we try to assist them.

It must be obvious from what I have said what kinds of mortals will attract the earthbound: Those who go in for alcoholism, narcotic addiction, gluttony, gambling or betting compulsively, cruelty, thievery, practicing black witchcraft, sex to excess, or similar iniquities. If you have these vices and do not care if you are aided and abetted as well as watched incessantly by a lawless type of spirit, then proceed at your own risk.

XII

SEX BETWEEN THE SPHERES

SEX IS ONE of the earthbound spirits' favorite subjects, so humans who indulge in promiscuous relations need feel no particular surprise to learn that they are being constantly observed by invisible Peeping Toms. If the idea bothers them, there is nothing to do about it except alter their habits. Despite current theories, free will does exist and must be used if one expects to live wisely and well.

Those whose minds are so engrossed with sexual gratification that they cannot live without it constantly, and usually with a variety of partners, have a difficult time when they first come over to the spirit world. They insist on continuing their old practices, and—knowing nothing about the power of thought, which allows more advanced spirits to participate in whatever activities they prefer—they can only do it vicariously, by watching mortals who are indulging. After a time these sex addicts may find someone with whom they can have actual physical sex relations; then, with sufficient psychic power coming from their earth partners, and with a strong desire on their own part, they may be able to make their presence felt. A spirit who takes out his lust on humans is invariably frustrated, but he will still feel it is better than nothing. Such an entity will undoubtedly not be familiar with the words "incubus" and "succubus," but these are what spirits attempting to fornicate with earth persons are traditionally called. An incubus is a male spirit who intrudes himself upon mortal women. A succubus is a woman spirit who has an interest in the male who is still in his physical form.

Now, it is perfectly true that a person who has lost a beloved mate may sometimes feel the spouse's presence in bed at night, and some do actually have an occasional experience of lovemaking. This is not to be decried, if it gives one reassurance. If you desire to make the effort, you may enjoy having the semblance of relations with an immaterial yet nonetheless potent visitor. I do not recommend it unless it is with your spouse, for it leads to emotional confusions and involvements of various sorts, all of which are completely undesirable. It has often been known throughout history, and is even now accepted by psychiatrists, that a woman sometimes believes herself to have a "demon lover" and is able to experience his caresses in quite a satisfactory manner. The doctors have always tried to relieve the woman of her misapprehensions, instead of eliminating the entity who, I now affirm, is actually present.

COMMENTARY:
The late Dr. Nandor Fodor, psychoanalyst and psychical researcher, in Between Two Worlds *describes what is probably most readers' feeling of revulsion at this concept: "The question of whether or not the living can be involved in the sexual desires of the dead is an absurd, terrifying, and obscene issue, apt to evoke frightful spectres of the Middle Ages that we have believed laid forever. And so no one was more surprised than I on finding out that these nightmare creatures still haunt the living whether as purely psychological entities within the mind of the afflicted or something bewilderingly more."*

I personally had also thought of these as only psychogenic problems. But after I wrote about such experiences in World of the Strange, *I began to receive letters from readers describing exactly what James says occurs. One woman who lives in Seattle, Washington, wrote me that she was awakened in the middle of the night in 1971 by an extremely sharp stab in her "nether parts." She wrote, "I could see some big black entity above me trying to enter my body. Being a very religious person I prayed and prayed hard . . . and it left. But it certainly gave me a terrific fright."*

Dr. Fodor, who was a friend of mine, treated a woman who had been involved with an incubus for several years. There was so much evidence of genuine manifestations, observed not only by the pa-

tient but by her mother as well, that he finally was forced to conclude that he had run into an actual instance of "something bewilderingly more" than a mere "psychological entity within the mind."

Even after I had talked to Dr. Fodor about his interesting case, I was hardly prepared for something similar when a woman wrote asking me to telephone her because she couldn't put the gruesome details in a letter. She had reached her unpleasant situation by communicating by automatic writing without protecting herself in advance—something James always warns against. For all those who are fortunate enough to have a good relationship with interesting spirit communicants, there are an occasional few who run into trouble. Since the entities are invisible, who can tell the good from the bad, until perhaps they have made unpleasant or indecent overtures? When I phoned this woman, the story she told was that her communicant had turned into an incubus about two years before and had attacked her. It had felt exactly as if she were being raped. Before that time she'd had a very happy disposition, she said, but she had it no longer, for her molester seldom let her alone.

The detailed account I received could not but make me suspect that the lady who wrote was suffering from emotional excitability, excessive anxiety, and any number of other psychiatric conditions. Had I not already known about incubi, I'm not sure just how I would have reacted to her story. Since I did know, however, what was the proper answer to give her when she asked how to protect herself? I frankly attacked both aspects of her problem. I suggested that she go to a psychiatrist I knew who was open to the possibility of spirit possession and that she also go to a medium. An analyst who understood her problem from both the scientific and the spiritistic point of view certainly would be the ideal person to help her cope with her problem. If he thought her incubus was only a mental aberration, he would probably be of no assistance whatever. A medium, or even, if the intruding spirit had a religious turn of mind, a priest, might be able to exorcise the incubus just as any other possessing or obsessing spirit may be exorcised; and this would be the best thing that could happen. Besides suggesting that she get all the outside help possible, I also told her to use James' techniques of visualizing herself surrounded with protection, and also to demand vociferously that the entity leave and bother her no more.

From their accounts I have not gathered that any of the people who have written me about having unwanted sexual experiences with spirits have been promiscuous, even though James suggests that this is the type who more frequently attract the unseen swingers.

After all, when we are dealing with medieval concepts that are still manifesting in the twentieth century, we are working in a definite problem area and I believe in taking all the precautions necessary. Certainly denying the existence of such manifestations is hardly the answer.

When we more advanced spirits see an earthbounder who is causing trouble to an individual who does not invite it, we will do everything we can to thwart his efforts and to divert his attention from his malicious acts . . . and thoughts. We talk to him and reason with him, and eventually we convince him that he is potentially good and will someday return to the God state as a perfected human being. If he were to hear from his victim that she is also aware of his need for assistance and is sorry for him and is praying for him, it could well startle him into leaving her alone. He would hardly be likely to thrust his unwelcome attentions on one who was in the midst of praying for his very soul. If he should continue, however, she should become very firm, saying aloud, "I will never pay attention to you again, so go away. I dislike you and everything you represent and will have nothing further to do with you. Please leave at once." Following that she visualizes herself wrapped in a protecting wall that is so solid he cannot penetrate it in any way and holds the thought at all times that nothing can come near her that does not come from God in love and peace. From all this the entity will certainly understand that he is not wanted and go away. Her efforts in his behalf will bore him if nothing else.

After all, you must always remember that those who attempt to possess, assault or in any other way influence you negatively are not demons or devils. They are only miserable misfits who know no better than to behave as they do. As you can imagine, it is not easy to convince them of their ability to improve themselves. They have never before had such an idea in their entire lives. That is why I am trying to tell you now that you are an immortal being . . . who comes from God and will return to God. Unless one has been indoctrinated with such a winning precept beforehand, changing him after his death is much more difficult.

A person who is involved with a human partner whom he truly loves is in no danger whatever from intruders. After all, what could possibly make them feel more unwelcome? But if you are sexually promiscuous, you may be attracting more than you anticipate. If this alarms you, it is possible to change your pattern of living so that it is less enticing to unseen fornicators.

Blindly ignoring or merely bemoaning the situation will not control it. But revising your own habits can modify your life so that you will not attract such evil spirits because you do not do the things that appeal to them. No one has to drift through life as he is. It is possible to make yourself into whatever you desire to be. If your thoughts are positive and uplifting, they will not interest those who might otherwise intrude upon you. If your life exhibits the finer virtues and you know how to protect yourself, you will have no one unseen to fight for the possession of your thoughts . . . or your body. The best way to keep such as these away from you is to be so clean living and positive thinking that you do not interest them in the least.

There is something about earthbound entities that does not like busy people. If you spend your time in interesting work that keeps you actively occupied with something constructive, you will not be bothered at all. Trying to improve your capabilities and talents by using them can keep you so happily occupied that your mind is seldom free to dwell on sensuality. Then you will not only be strengthening yourself but you will also be discouraging intruders.

Now, let me assure you that I am not trying to frighten you. Neither do I wish to make sanctimonious souls out of you. Happiness should be the natural state of man, and happiness would be your lot on earth if everyone were aware that he is immortal and so lived. There would be no wars, no slums, no need for jails, if each held the welfare of others above his own. Yet lending a helping hand does not keep you from enjoying yourself, and certainly need not make you pious and dull. Many delightful occupations and pastimes may busy you even though you are able to keep your thoughts under control. The most charming, fulfilled and joyous people on earth are those whose lives are dedicated to others.

XIII

ANGELS AND GODS ARE REAL

Yes, Angels and gods really do exist. They are people, just as you and I are, but people in the tremendously advanced stages of near perfection and actual perfection. It should be inspiring for you to realize that you, too, will someday reach such an exalted peak in your development. Everyone will.

The use of the characterizations "angels" and "gods" may seem quaint, but they are familiar words so we will continue to employ them for the most highly advanced states. I could use other general terms, such as masters, avatars, mentors, etc., but I prefer not to, for they have different meanings to different peoples. We also have semantic problems with "angels" and "gods," as can well be understood; however, they are the best words available and so I will use them.

Commentary:
Almost all the material in this chapter was received from James with the rest of this manuscript in 1967. I have witnesses to that fact —friends who read and discussed it with me at the time. I was actually rather embarrassed about this business of angels and gods as I read what rolled from my fingers onto the typewriter. I thought it was entirely a mythological concept, and indeed in my limited metaphysical reading experience it was.

Imagine my surprise in the summer of 1973 to find in Dr. Gina

Cerminara's new book Insights for the Age of Aquarius *a chapter called* "Hierarchy, Angels, and Gods." *Dr. Cerminara writes:*

"To assume . . . that God is directly above ourselves, with no intermediate intelligences in between, is a very large assumption. And to assume that any seemingly strange or supernatural phenomenon must necessarily have been produced by the Supreme Godhead of all the Universe is an equally large assumption. Yet these two assumptions are very widespread, and they lead to many serious confusions."

On our planet there are thousands of different kinds of creatures, from tiny one-celled forms on up, Dr. Cerminara points out. When studying these creatures, we observe many finely gradated steps of structure, from the simple to the complex, and many finely gradated steps of intelligence. Why, then, she asks, should we assume that these steps reach their highest point at man? "Wouldn't it be more logical to assume that the sequence continues beyond man, in a hierarchy of form, intelligence, and consciousness that may not be visible to man but nonetheless real?"

For all its plausibility this idea is certainly not current in the twentieth century. Various discoveries of modern physics have made us aware of the reality of invisible waves and forces, and of frequency bands of light, sound, and energy far beyond the range of our senses. "But," says Dr. Cerminara, "this awareness has not for the most part led people to think of the possibility of invisible and superior beings who may be functioning in these higher frequencies."

She reminds us, however, that the idea has been seriously considered since earliest times by many people, not merely by primitive tribes—given, as we think, to superstition—but by some of the finest intellects in the spheres of philosophy, science, and religion. Many Greek philosophers, among whom were Aristotle, Plato, Pythagoras, and the neo-Platonists, expressed belief in a succession of intelligences between God and man. "The philosopher-historian Plutarch felt, in fact, that it was absurd to think otherwise."

It encouraged me to see what good support Dr. Cerminara gives to the theory of angels and gods. No matter how naïve it may appear to modern readers, the ideas are sensible, she maintains, for "Wherever we see a successfully functioning organization—the *army, government, big business, large churches, universities—we see a hierarchical system in operation: people in graded ranks with authority delegated to them from higher levels in the scale. It is logical, then, to infer that a similar hierarchy could exist for the running of the vast organization which we call the universe."*

Most of the religions of the world, Dr. Cerminara points out, have accepted the idea of higher beings, intermediate between man and God. They have invariably been referred to in terms meaning either angels or gods. She says: "Modern educated persons usually regard angels and gods as a superstitious relic of ignorant ages, but perhaps the whole idea deserves to be re-examined."

Every angel and every god was once a human being. He may not have lived on your planet, but that does not matter. In the advanced spheres of the universe the various planets and their inhabitants are to progressed spirits just like people who live in another town or another country are to you. They gather together on any occasion when it is necessary. No place is far away to them, for they travel back and forth by the power of thought. Gods are angels who have improved themselves even more and are at the point of personal achievement where they are actually aware at all times of their great and wonderful union with Ultimate Perfection.

COMMENTARY:

Because so many who accept the angels of the Bible believe that they are special beings created individually by God independently from man, a reader has questioned James' idea that those in the higher echelons, to borrow a phrase from Gina Cerminara, advanced upward from the ranks. Gina, too, has noted this distinction, saying: "Different opinions have been held on this point even by distinguished seers. Swedenborg, for example, was emphatic that all angels had first been human beings. Jacob Boehme was equally insistent that God created the angels directly, out of Himself."

Perhaps the Old Testament angels can be construed as God's independent creations, but in the New Testament there is apparently a different connotation. In Matthew, Chapter 18, Jesus called a little child to him and set him in the midst of them and said (18:

10), "*Take heed that ye despise not one of these little ones; for I say unto you, that in heaven their angels do always behold the face of my Father which is in heaven.*"

As this is translated, how can it mean anything other than that the child becomes an angel and sees God? That is just what James is saying.

No advanced spirits, most particularly not those who have achieved the state of angels and gods, ever come back and live again on earth in order to be spiritual leaders. It should be much more inspiring for you to realize that actual men have achieved during one lifetime on earth such states of love and fulfillment as the great leaders have shown in their exemplary lives. The angels and gods assist mankind, instead, from their side of the veil, by making special events occur to aid you and in other ways accomplishing things a mere human or a spirit in the lower levels would be unable to do. When what seems to you to be a miracle occurs, expect an angel to be back of it.

Angels and gods have numerous duties. As I have said before, life would never be endurable for long periods of time unless one had constructive work to do. Pleasurable activities of all kinds are going on constantly throughout spirit life, but we couldn't spend all our time just enjoying ourselves without a true goal of achievement—and this is what I mean by work. There is so much that is fascinating in it, however, that it is never an irksome chore. It is exciting, challenging and inspiring.

At the highest level gods' occupations consist of such activity as forming new galaxies or inventing an original type of insect or animal for an already existing but newly developing planet. Think of the fun it must be to dream up some novel creature that is going to be reproduced in matter and live in a physical body in some new world! This shouldn't seem too preposterous to those who have advanced in their thinking beyond the idea that everything happens by chance or by natural selection. And certainly no one who is reading these words still believes that an anthropomorphic god with a long white beard accomplishes it all with a wave of his hand. So how do you suppose it gets done? By the conscious thoughts and inventions of that aspect of Divine Consciousness known as gods.

All the animals, trees, flowers, insects . . . all life of every kind that exists on our planet was consciously devised by highly developed spirits who came originally from other inhabited planets. It was a great challenge to them to put new forms of existence on this ball of dirt when it had attained the proper conditions so that life could be sustained.

Many gods, I am told, are today evolving new worlds and inventing life forms for planets which come to a state of readiness for them. Those who are not so occupied have other duties . . . a great many of which I haven't learned yet. They leave most of the problems on their home planets to the angels and to spirits in various stages of advancement.

Angels do become personally involved with you on earth. People who believe that Jesus is ever at their beck and call, or that God is personally taking a hand in their problems, are actually receiving assistance from angels. Yet because they are humans who have developed to the point that they fully understand their oneness with God, angels are actual facets of the God-mind, or, if you wish, the Christ-spirit. And so the Divine Consciousness is participating here through the activity of its aspect known as angels.

Angels do spend much of their time assisting mortals. If you call for them, they will come, and you will see the results of their efforts in short order. If you are psychic, or in an especially receptive condition, there is even the rare possibility that you may see one of them, usually as a vision in human form, which you interpret as a saint or a visitation from your deity, whoever he is.

COMMENTARY:
There is a young sidereal astrologer in San Francisco who calls himself Count Gramalkin. Recently when I was talking with him, he expressed the firm conviction that angels exist and will help human beings if we will call for their aid when we need it. I told him James said the same thing. He then relayed to me the proper ground rules for getting assistance from angels, as he had learned them from his teacher. I thought them so charming that I wrote them down, and later asked James if I could use them in this book. My mentor said they were actually quite accurate and gave his permission for them to be quoted herewith.

Ground Rules for Calling Angels

1. *You have to ask for help to get it. We all have free will, you know.*
2. *Don't tell angels their business. Just ask them to watch over, guide and comfort you; then leave it up to them.*
3. *They like formality when there is time. In an emergency situation just a cry for help will do.*
4. *Ask them to please stay until the situation is taken care of.*
5. *If someone else in whom you are interested needs assistance, you can send angels to them if they wouldn't be likely to ask for themselves.*
6. *Don't cry wolf. Never call for angels unless you really need them desperately.*
7. *And always say thank you.*

I was quite surprised that Gramalkin knew about angels, for so few people do. He told me he had frequently appealed to them and that he had psychically seen them coming to his aid. He described them as actually sailing in on large white feathery wings; but I'm sure he must have gotten his angels mixed up with Jonathan Livingston Seagull's. I told him James would definitely not describe them that way, as they are still the spirits of people. Where in their transition upward would they manage to acquire the wings of birds? When I returned home to my typewriter, I asked James about this. He wrote:

The only thing really inaccurate about Gramalkin's information is that he visualized angels with wings of feathers. No doubt they so appeared to him because that is the way he expected them to look. Many things you see are so colored by your beliefs that they appear to you with configurations of your own creation. When any of us on our plane see angels, it is as great glowing lights. They have progressed so far that they pulsate at such a high frequency that spirits on lower levels are unable to see them most of the time. And you on earth see them on very rare occasions.

It is true that when an angel appears to you in the guise of a human, which is exactly how he looks when his frequency is lowered to earth's density, you almost invariably take him to be the specific god or saint you might expect to see. Whoever you think he is, realize that he has gone to a great deal of effort to slow down the atomic motion of his organism so that he can make an appearance in the heavier earth atmosphere. Angels come in human form because they do not want you to think of them as remote seraphic beings. They still know themselves to be people and do not wish to be dehumanized in your thoughts. They would prefer that you regard them as loving brothers or sisters.

You may, as I have said, have a guardian angel of your own who is advancing in the Astral plane. But in times of great trouble or need you can appeal to other angels as well and they will come to you. They may have no such personal interest in you as your guardian angel does, except that they love you because you are an incipient angel yourself and will one day be one of them. But because of their great humanitarian feeling, they want to help you, and will do all they can for you when you call on them. So petition the angels whenever you are in bad trouble of any kind, and then make yourself receptive to their assistance. They will come.

It may seem strange to some of you that Supreme Intelligence does not consciously take action itself to help mankind. You have probably always hoped there is a personal God and feel that what I have said here indicates there is not. There *is* a personal God. Divine Consciousness is involved with everything, but in the person of its units of operation—which are the angels and gods. You are as much a part of God as they are, but you do not know it. Even those of you on earth who meditate the most and are most aware of your true identification with divinity are able to concentrate on it for only occasional minutes of time. Angels and gods have progressed to the point where they are aware of this unity every moment. That is why it is possible for them knowingly to do God's will. It is for Him that they come to you on earth and help you when you call out. It is for you, also, for each one of you is beloved by each one of them.

If you are of such personal concern to God, then, you often wonder why he allows such tragedies and unhappiness to happen to you. This is a common complaint of those who are living in human bodies and trying to cope with the many trials of an earthly existence. And it is quite understandable. But nothing that occurs to you is deliberately planned or foreordained; and you do have free will.

The law of cause and effect is in operation at all times and when you take certain steps or think certain thoughts, you create certain results. This is inevitable. What happens to you is not consequential, however, as I am sure you have already grasped by now. What is of consequence is what you learn from it. All you are on earth for is to start the evolutionary process of your existence that will continue forever in conscious awareness of your identity. The kind of start you get is very important, but only within yourself, as it affects your development as a person.

All the gods and angels are aware of this, knowing that whatever you can learn on earth you will not have to learn in the spirit world. Their view of your ultimate destiny is as comprehensive as your view would be of the human growth potential of your baby. Thus gods and angels do not become anguished over any tragic circumstance that occurs in your life any more than you would cry if your baby stubs his toe. They understand its relationship to your overall long-term life experience just as you are aware of the insignificance of a tiny tripping.

It is to angels that we must eventually look to solve the problem of some earthbound spirits who have been in their desperate straits much too long. After having ignored all succor from those missionaries who spend hours and days and even years endeavoring to pick them up and put them on their feet, there comes a time when they are ultimately turned over to the angels. No matter how depraved a spirit might be, when he sees a vision of glowing light and beauty who gives him an inspirational talk, he will listen. For this reason I am able to state that no soul is ever lost for all time. Supreme Intelligence will not allow any part of himself to be thrown away permanently. He wants it all back. Eventually some angel will be able to convert the earthbound entity from his degraded ways and start him on the right path. None is so corrupt that an actual visitation by an entity of eminence will not straighten him out and head him in the proper direction. But everything else that can possibly be done is tried first. If angels went after every earthbound spirit except as a last resort, they would have time to accomplish nothing else.

It takes angels a great deal of effort to reduce their frequencies to the point that their presence can be seen and felt on the lower astral levels. It is even more difficult for them to make themselves visible to you on earth, and that is one of the reasons angels are so seldom on view. Yet even the highest of all advanced souls have on occasion undertaken this task for the sake of some earthly petitioner. I do not in the least doubt that Jesus Christ has appeared to many of those who claim to have seen him. The Buddha is sometimes available also, and many others of magnitude.

Personally, if I were living on earth at the present time and knew what I know now, I would be calling on the angels constantly. I would start clubs and organizations all over the world for the purpose of involving as many people as possible in a great campaign of prayer for assistance. You are at a very low point right now in your history because you are all so depressed about so many things.

We have not given up on you, however. We know what the destiny of earth is, and it is great. You will not go down in flames nor blow up in atomic blasts. Neither will you overpopulate yourselves to extinction or let everyone starve to death. With your technology and your awakening interest in your fellow men, you will come out all right eventually. What you call the dawning Age of Aquarius will be a period of enlightenment. But right now conditions for almost everyone in almost every area of the world are so negative—and as your young people say, "The vibes are so bad"—that you must do something about them in order to progress at the pace necessary. You are in a very low spiritual slump, so start taking the proper steps to get out of it. Begin your positive thinking on a massive scale, working hard to convince everyone how necessary it is. And . . . call the angels!

XIV

BABIES COME AND BABIES GO

A CHILD COMES into the world with the Soul, or Consciousness, he has inherited from God and the body and capabilities he has inherited from his ancestors. And the consciousness becomes manifest at birth, not a moment before. The spirit body is the pattern around which the physical body grows in the womb; but there is no conscious awareness within either body until birth. The fetus is a lively little organism that lives, grows and reacts to physical stimuli, but it does not think. It is the mother's subconscious mind that controls its function as long as it is a part of her body. The memories some people believe they have of events that occurred during their time in the womb are retrocognitive psychic impressions only and do not represent the activity of any kind of mental process before birth.

COMMENTARY:

The night after I received the above paragraph I was lying in bed thinking about it: "Yes, but some people say the consciousness arrives at conception, and some say it arrives at the quickening . . . about twelve weeks after conception. I wonder why it is better to have it arrive at birth."

As this was going through my mind, I had an urge to get up and rush to my typewriter, and the following appeared:

"If you want to give me an argument about this, I have one or two answers. You know, if you stop to think about it, that no mind could *endure to be confined in such a small dark space as a womb for nine months. Why, the baby would come out of it with inborn claustrophobia it would never get over."*

"But the fetus may be sleeping," I suggested.

James replied, *"If a consciousness were in the baby during its fetal period, and if the system had it so arranged that it would spend most of its nine months in utero sleeping, a habit pattern would be so programmed into it that it would be difficult for it to keep awake for the rest of its life."*

There was no use my arguing anymore, even if I had thought of anything else to say, for James concluded briskly, *"No, the arrival of the consciousness at birth is much more logical. And, anyway, it is factual."*

When a new baby is born, its forbears who are interested in it gather around to help it enter the world just as we also frequently assemble to greet the soul leaving the physical body at death, when it is born into the spirit world.

The genes the child has from his parents and grandparents and other progenitors determine his physical and mental makeup. He is not discriminated against by an avenging God if he is born without good health or a good brain through which his mind can operate. It is his inheritance from his ancestors plus what happens to him during his fetal period. His consciousness is always sound, but if the brain is defective the consciousness cannot function through it normally. And thus we have those poor little creatures called imbeciles or morons. A reincarnationist would say that it is not fair unless they will have another chance to live another, more successful, life on earth. But this is not necessary, for they are handicapped only while in their physical bodies. After death they will have the same opportunities as anybody else. Cause and effect—bad heritage, illness, damage, or lack of proper bodily elements in the mother—caused the brain of the baby to be so poorly constructed that its consciousness (which is perfectly normal) is not able to function through it in order to communicate adequately with the world. The individual with nothing to use but this unfortunate mechanism will not progress much on earth, to be sure, and most of his time there will be wasted. When liberated from the body at death he has a good bit of catching up to do. But in the spirit world he will be cared for, loved and taught in much the same way as babies are who die. He will have all the opportunities to learn and grow spiritually that they do. And his progress will be no slower than theirs. Eventually he will arrive at his heavenly destination just as everyone else does.

Divine Consciousness does not change or abrogate the law of cause and effect so that a baby can be born perfectly normal if, say, its mother suffers German measles early in her pregnancy. Neither can the law be changed so that a child who happens to fall from its crib and break its neck will not die of injuries. These are among the tragic hardships of existence and can only be borne, until the time comes when a preventative is found for German measles and all cribs are so constructed that no baby can fall out of them. However, the system also has provided that babies grow up in the spirit world with loving care, and that each one can have a good and eventful life in the Astral plane of existence, achieving whatever fulfillment he did not find on earth. Every individual will eventually attain Ultimate Perfection, no matter what causes and effects have delayed him or made his start different from the norm.

If you are not happy with a system in which some children are born mentally or physically handicapped, then see to it that those adults who are not properly equipped to bear offspring are prohibited from doing so. In a world which has the problem of overpopulation—or in any world, for that matter—sterilization of the unfit is only logical and proper. You people on earth will come to it some day. You should also make sure that the mother is well during the time she is carrying her baby. If she contracts German measles or other diseases that will affect the fetus or takes medicine that will harm its brain then she should abort the child. It is important that only babies are allowed to be born who have a healthy mind and a heritage of good genes that will make them mentally able to cope with life. As soon as you are a matured civilization, you will know enough to make this a legal requirement. Once you accept the fact that no baby has a sense of awareness until birth, you will be able to consider the idea of abortion without so many qualms. Abortion does not remove a conscious human being. It is no more the taking of a life than removal of a tumor would be.

No infant should come into the world who does not have the ability to become a mentally self-sustaining, successful individual. It is difficult for parents to make the decision to abort a prospective offspring who is sure to be defective, but it is much more difficult for them to raise a handicapped child. Many parents have spent their lives in misery just because they have given birth to an imperfect infant.

However, a parent who loves and cares for a child who is unable to cope with life on his own learns a great deal and has the opportunity for much character development. It is those who dismiss such children to institutions and then forget about them as quickly as possible who are at fault. I do not mean that it is wrong for a family to hospitalize a deficient baby. Definitely not. In many institutions they receive better care than they could get at home. I denigrate only those who do not visit the child, never admit its existence, try to dismiss it from their lives. They are the ones who learn nothing from their problem, shunning it and depositing an unwanted and incompetent offspring on a world that has to take care of it. These parents have a definite responsibility toward this infant nonetheless, and after death they must assist it to learn all the things it was unable to learn on earth because of its flawed mind. (Parents do not have the same responsibility for an aborted fetus, for it did not have a Soul to survive death.) It will not be difficult for a former mental defective in the Etheric, for he will no longer be blemished. No matter what his age at death, he will be cared for in the spirit world the same as a baby who dies in infancy, having wise and loving teachers. He will then learn about life in the way that they learn, for he is as teachable as anyone else.

All babies are raised in the Astral in joyous conditions and are well trained by spirits who have lost a child while on earth and longed for it, or who never had children and wish to raise some. A child grows up after death just as he does on earth. The spirit body, which is the pattern, is intact at death and is able to grow in the spirit world just as it would have grown on earth in conjunction with the physical body. There is no real problem of an eternal nature that is engendered by a child's being defective or by dying young. And the life of a baby raised in the spirit world is much happier than if he had grown up on earth. He has more to learn, in some ways, because he is not subject to the buffetings he would normally have to undergo, which can help very much in building character.

Still, he can experience vicariously the problems of his family, for he is raised with it—yes, you did not know that, did you? The tot is not taken away from you when he dies. He lives right in your vicinity, cared for by loving spirits, but frequently in sight of you. If he is old enough to observe, he may wonder why you are grieving, and for a long time it is difficult to explain to him why his parents and siblings do not talk to him and include him in their activities; but eventually he understands. The spirit playmates of earth children may often be their own brothers and sisters who have passed over.

Each child who dies is raised in the spirit world with love and understanding. It could be considered fortunate to die young, except for the fact that the lessons one would have learned on earth must now be acquired from a different point of view, which makes for some difficulty. He does not have to undergo the heartaches and hardships of life, the emotional frustrations that beset us all, and the problem of trying to understand what life is all about. He gains his personal sense of values, his honor, integrity, and moral responsibility by observation, as it were, rather than by actual experience. Many who grow up in the Astral progress rapidly, but some find certain aspects more complicated this way than they might have found them if they had lived their lives on earth.

The parents of a child who has died should never try to put it out of their thoughts in order to keep from suffering over it. Since it will be raised right with them, they should talk to it occasionally and let it know they still love and remember it. Do not grieve excessively for anyone who has died; but include him in your lives as much as possible, even though he is now invisible to you. If your friends look at you askance when you speak aloud to your lost infant, tell them you know it still to be there in spirit form and then let the matter drop. Do not argue with anyone about it. There is no use in letting yourself be considered unbalanced by your family and friends; but at the same time if you will talk to your deceased child you will be maintaining the warm relationship that will be resumed when you join it at your passing into its realm. Perhaps, on second thought, it might be best to hold these conversations when you are alone, with no human to misjudge your actions.

If you become truly aware of the truth of what I am saying, you may learn to sense your child's presence. Some who have developed their own psychic powers have had actual communication with their dead children. Some parents who have lost a baby are conscious at all times of its presence with them. In fact some psychic individuals are aware most of the time of the kindly invisible associates who are so often in their homes. If they are, their lives are invariably more peaceful than those who blindly grieve without any hope of ever seeing the loved one again. If you will continue to think of your child who has died, it will inevitably feel close to you as it grows to adulthood in its spirit body in the beautiful world of the Astral.

XV

REINCARNATION

MANY PEOPLE TODAY feel that if you accept a theory of evolutionary progressive existence after death, you have to believe in reincarnation. Those who have rejected orthodoxy presume they have no place to go except to the ancient doctrine of many lives in physical bodies on earth. Evolutionary Soul Progression is a third alternative, however. To some it may not at first be as attractive an idea; but it is so logical that many who are flirting with reincarnation because they do not know what else to believe will be highly gratified to find out about it.

Reincarnation has more followers than any other doctrine, having had its origin long ago in the highly populous countries of the Orient. It is rare to find any two persons who interpret it in exactly the same way, as there are almost as many reincarnation beliefs as believers. The Yoga concept, more prevalent in the East, is that one has to keep spinning on the Wheel of Life until he sees the illusory nature of earthly desires and achieves complete selflessness. Only then can he escape the cycle of earthly rebirths and achieve nirvana. More often accepted in the West, on the other hand, is the idea that in order to fulfill himself each individual needs to live many times on earth so that he can learn every kind of lesson from having all types of experiences.

The theory that one is given opportunities to accomplish in other lives what he was unable to achieve the first time around is appealing; and many wonderful people who are sincerely seeking enlightenment are intrigued by it. As I have already shown, though, when one understands Evolutionary Soul Progression he realizes that undergoing more than one life in order to learn is unnecessary. If it is not known that we progress in spirit spheres, then naturally there must be some other intelligent means to continue to live and learn, and the idea of going through numerous lives has strong romantic appeal. It is certainly glamorous to picture yourself as having been an Egyptian king or a Chinese concubine, a great Persian warrior, or even a slave in the Golden Age of Greece.

Because it seems to explain all of life's inequalities, the idea of "karma" has especial appeal, for karma gives you the opportunity to make retribution for your past sins of omission or commission. Adherents to the theory of reincarnation believe that your situation in your present life is your personal choice in order to improve conditions that existed in previous lives when you made mistakes or committed crimes and did nothing to correct them. If you were a dissolute Roman emperor, for instance, who caused human beings to die at your whim, you now choose to enter the body of a poor and perhaps deformed baby so that you must suffer intolerable unhappiness. If you blinded men during the Inquisition, when you had a position of authority, you may now come back to earth as a sightless child in order to make recompense.

As you have read this book you have already begun to understand the Evolutionary Progressionists' answer to how karma can be worked off after death, when by your conscious effort at self-improvement you learn compassion, tolerance, integrity, responsibility, and all the other virtues you have missed acquiring. You may also have seen that the inequalities of life, which are among the main complaints of reincarnationists, are actually opportunities to learn, not punishments.

You have also by now realized how unimportant the conditions of physical existence are in the overall picture. Life on earth is primarily for establishing your identity. Whatever else of value you acquire from it is an asset, but it can be experienced in the spirit world after death if it has not been learned on earth, as witness the progress of those who die in infancy. Of course, it is right and proper to have a good earth life, and the more you learn from it the farther ahead you are after death; but it is not essential to your ultimate progress. It is not necessary that you make up on earth *in another life* for things you have not acquired or undergone or learned in this one. This only seems important when it *is* not understood that existence in the earliest phases of the Etheric plane is very similar to existence on earth. It is during this time of gradual transition that all recompense is made for errors committed, and as you progress all opportunities longed for are experienced.

Naturally to you life on earth seems lengthy while you are living it, and each event is terribly important. Because you have a limited viewpoint of the overall picture, this is to be expected. But actually in the wider perspective your life on earth is extremely short. In fact, of your entire eternal existence the period that is spent on earth is roughly equal in comparative length to the first mile in a trip around the world. And you certainly would not wish to return and retravel that first mile over and over again before you went on with the rest of your tour.

You want to do the best you can with your time on earth, and so you hope for the type of experiences that will give you the most successful basis for the future. You would not wish to start your trip around the world with no preparation; neither will you want to begin your journey ahead in life ill prepared. But surely you can see the unimportance of each specific event that happens to you in such a relatively short period of time. It is what you do with the situation in which you find yourself that is of value.

COMMENTARY:
Emanuel Swedenborg, who says that every soul is a new creation who had not preexisted, also states that the spirit is real and the spiritual world is real—a world in which a full, rich, human life can be enjoyed. Our life on earth is a temporary, but important phase of our existence; the prelude to endless, uninterrupted life in the spiritual world, our true home.

When civilization has reached such a state of development that each person will be so responsible for his actions that nothing occurs that is not causative of good effects, then all men will be born beautiful, strong, and whole, mentally and physically, and their lives will be happy throughout. Even now as each year passes it can be seen that experimentally, scientifically, medically, man is attempting to reach toward utopia. Although you may tend to doubt it, in the area of human relations progress now is more rapid than at any time in the history of the world. In your current civil rights movements, ecology activities, your concerned young people, your efforts to emancipate women and to alleviate overcrowded cities and improve slum conditions you are today showing great forward movement. Less than one hundred twenty-five years ago slavery was accepted as proper by the majority; today the need for improved status for blacks is a hot issue sponsored by many millions of whites. Consider the plight of the insane one hundred fifty years ago, when they were treated as criminals and chained in prisons. Granted that conditions in institutions are not now nearly as good as they should be, the improvement in general attitude toward the insane is noticeable. And it is only in this century that child labor laws have been passed.

So there are obvious indications that some of you are becoming aware of your fellow men and their needs. When the great spiritual revolution in man's thinking comes and he is able to lift his brothers to the high levels to which he himself aspires, then your life will reach a true utopian state. The ideal is still a long way off; and many millions of men and women will suffer tribulations before it arrives. If earth life were all there is, then this anguish would have been in vain. Fortunately earthly existence is such a small part of all life that the suffering one undergoes here is soon overlooked when progression begins. Do not forget that earth is only the first short mile in the journey to Ultimate Perfection.

So keep in mind that it does not matter what problems you encounter in life. As I said earlier, the angels with their wisdom will not cry any more over your suffering than you would cry if your baby stubbed his toe. What is important is how you overcome your problems and what you learn from them. There is no reason to believe that you must undergo all varieties of experience. It is possible to learn in one lifetime on earth enough about good and evil to give you a start toward obtaining wisdom. You will learn everything else you need to know during the eons of time you progress in the spirit world.

System always prevails in God's universe. The laws of cause and effect are in operation at all times, and they constantly govern the activities of everything occurring on your earth as well as the rest of the cosmos. Whenever a cause exists, an effect inevitably follows. And so the system ordains that man comes into the world as a baby with a mind, a spiritual body and a physical body. His ability to use his mind depends on the body's physical condition. The extent of his talents and capabilities is based on his heritage from his ancestors. Inheritance is a fantastically complicated and interesting thing, for it encompasses much more than just the color of one's hair and eyes and the shape of his nose. Racial memories are inherited not only from parents and grandparents, but also from many generations past. The memories some people have of an occasional past life can well be those of any of his forebears.

COMMENTARY:

Discussing the existence of concentrations of RNA (ribonucleic acid) in brain cells, Isaac Asimov in Is Anyone There? *says: "There is no question . . . but that the RNA molecule represents a filing system perfectly capable of handling any load of learning and memory that the human being is likely to put upon it—and a billion times more than that quantity, too." But, he adds, "One can't consider RNA molecules by themselves. They come from somewhere. It is known, for instance, that specific RNA molecules are formed as 'copies' of similar but even more complicated molecules, called DNA, in the cell nucleus. . . . The DNA molecules make up the genes, or units of heredity, and these are passed along from parents to offspring by means of a complex but nearly foolproof mechanism."*

This would mean, he says, that each person "carries a vast supply of possible memories, a 'memory bank,' so to speak, in the DNA molecules he was born with—a supply vast enough to take care of all reasonable contingencies."

Might this suggest, perhaps, that modern experimental science is beginning to explain Carl Jung's "racial unconscious"?

Harold Sherman, a prolific author who is also a highly talented sensitive, says in Psychic, *February, 1974: "I used to think that the concept of reincarnation explained the otherwise unexplainable. But as time went on and my experience became expanded, I began to see other possible alternatives. I began to realize we're just beginning to get into the study of genetics and genes and the physical characteristics our ancestors passed on to us. So why, then, if we ac-*

cept this, can't we accept the possibility that mental and emotional characteristics were also passed on through the genes?"

Purported memories of a past life could then sometimes be "recalled experiences which happened to a direct line ancestor. The mind is a highly imaginative tool and people, under suggestion or hypnosis, can easily dream up what they think they were or would like others to think they were."

There are many seers today who will tell you from a past life reading or from your astrological chart or some other means of fixation of their attention on your personal problems that you chose the parents you have because they have the proper "frequencies" or specific attributes, or even problems, for your present needs. You may be given much information about your characteristics and potentialities that is quite interestingly accurate. For this reason you are naturally tempted to accept the psychic's contention that he is giving you information he learned from one or more of your past lives. When it is recognized that persons who produce such information are putting into their interpretations what they are perhaps unconsciously gleaning from you clairvoyantly or telepathically, you can better understand the true situation. Naturally from what they learn psychically about you they are able to make suggestions and recommendations suitable to your problems.

Here is the especially salient point to keep in mind—which will clarify the reason that living many lives on earth would cause endless confusion. It is your conscious awareness of yourself as an individual that survives. This is an altogether different thing from the beliefs of the occultists that the reincarnating principle is an Atman, Over-Soul, Sutratma, Monad, ego, or essence. The modern parapsychologists call this surviving principle a psi-component or psychogenic factor. Seldom is it accepted that it could be anything so commonplace as the consciousness. The general idea is, then, that this something that continues to have an eternal existence merely plays the role of different individuals in different incarnations until it finally realizes that flesh is unimportant and that lives on earth are only illusion. After this it is willing to relinquish the cycle of rebirth.

What you are instead is an integrated whole, which can be identified as your personality, character, memories, and consciousness

—your awareness of yourself as an individual. Conscious awareness and memory are the keys here. Your memories constitute a large part of your personality and character, and thus of your actual identity.

COMMENTARY:

In 1919 Dr. James H. Hyslop, professor of logic and ethics at Columbia University and one of the founders of the American Society for Psychical Research wrote: ". . . reincarnation . . . does not satisfy the only instinct that makes survival of any kind interesting, namely the instinct to preserve the consciousness of personal identity. . . . A future life must be the continuity of this consciousness or it is not a life to us at all. . . ."

It would not be possible for anyone to live a number of lives as different people and come out of it still aware of his personal identity. It is easy to say that he lives the different lives as if he were in progressing grades at school, but this is not the way the system works. When one goes through school, he always retains his awareness of himself as the same individual, even though many of his aspects change as he grows and develops. When one is living a life he *is* that person, he is not just playing a role or a series of roles; so if he were to go through the lifetimes of a variety of different people, he would end up completely confused about his identity.

Now, after having discussed why it is not wise for a person to live more than one life, and what a problem it would be if he did so, I must state that, unfortunately, some people *do* live two lives . . . to their utter bewilderment at the end of their second experience. A spirit who believes he must reincarnate has occasionally moved into the body of a baby just before or just after it is born and has lived the life that should have belonged to the consciousness destined for that body. When the time comes for this second individual to die, the spirit who has lived both lives is entirely mixed-up. I have personally seen the evidence of this in several confused spirits who have undergone the anguish of trying to straighten out their identities after living two lives. It is terribly confusing for them to understand who and what they really are, for there has been no role-playing but the actual reality of *being* two different people. Those who idealize the idea of living many lives suspect that it will be easy, by some kind of simple process that goes on during the period between lifetimes, to encompass all the experiences and memories of various existences; but instead it is most difficult.

In the realm of memory alone you would be completely swamped.

COMMENTARY:
Isaac Asimov says in Is Anyone There? *"Some estimates are that the brain, in a lifetime, absorbs as many as one quadrillion— 1,000,000,000,000,000—separate bits of information."*

Memories are not always available to you on earth, and this is good because you would be overpowered by them. However, after your death all memories of everything that has ever in any way come in contact with either your mind or your body are intact and you can get at them. When the time comes that you begin to evaluate your life for the purpose of seeing what you must do to make amends for your omissions and commissions, you will review your time on earth, and all your memories of each event are available for this research.

Now, take into consideration the fact that not only are the interesting and important occurrences recallable after death, but everything else that has ever happened to you. All your thoughts and emotions are recorded in memory, also your night dreams and your daydreams, every word of every language you know, all the mathematical problems you have ever performed, and everything you studied in school and thought you had forgotten. It is bad enough to have to cope with the memories of one lifetime. Imagine how complicated it would be to have to face those of two or more lives and sort them out and try to get them straight. It is so befuddling that you can't even conceive of it.

Now let us consider one other aspect of the concept of reincarnation that makes it a very negative and unproductive philosophy: People who believe they must spin around and around on a Wheel of Life, never able to stop until they finally learn how to achieve complete selflessness, or perfection, or the nirvana state—however they interpret their goals—will accept whatever social conditions they find themselves in as their karma. Thus the Untouchables of India never made any effort to throw off their unbearable caste system, believing as they did that such a condition was their choice in order to work off karma from bad acts in former lives. One or two uprisings would have removed the stigma of this terrible social system long ago. But the lower castes would not try to change their situation because they thought it to be their own responsibility that they were where they were.

Actually, if the idea of karma were true, those who attempt to improve the lot of mankind would have no right even to help the poor or the miserable, for it is their karma to be in the state they are in and they should be allowed to suffer as they have chosen to suffer. So all the good that has been done for others in the world has instead foiled their efforts to improve themselves by living in a wretched state. Even easily remedied situations should not be alleviated, according to this, because they are karma. The person who has the problem chose it in order to learn certain lessons, and he should not be circumvented in his desires.

Much more could be said, if I were really making an effort to convince; but this is not a book to pressure anybody.

Instead I will conclude this chapter with a story that to me completes the picture tidily. It is an experience of Miss Susy Smith's. She had never held strong personal opinions either for or against reincarnation until she became the recipient of my communications. As long ago as 1956 I started right off telling her that she must not advocate it. She questioned me frequently about it as she discussed it often with her friends, many of whom are ardent enthusiasts of rebirth. She considered their viewpoints carefully because she had not yet received enough information from me about Evolutionary Soul Progression actually to be committed to it. Now, as this material flows through her fingers, she understands fully that reincarnation has no appeal for her; but whenever possible she avoids discussions with those who believe in it. She frankly says the subject bores her, for so many believers try to get her into arguments about it wherever she goes.

One day Susy was talking to a man who was determined to convince her that many lives were necessary. Nothing could swerve him from this, and he was one of those individuals who does not hesitate to use the supercilious bromide, "Well, when you are *ready*, you will see that reincarnation is the right doctrine." As the discussion continued, he began to insist that the fact that Susy is lame is due to karma. She is fully aware that her lameness resulted from an infection and an operation on her hip many years ago—although she has received from reincarnationists dozens of different "past life" explanations for it. By enduring her handicap with fortitude, Susy has developed more strength of character than she might have had occasion to acquire without the hip condition. However, this man was insisting that she had her problem because in some past life she had undoubtedly kicked someone into a lake and drowned him, or struck someone with her foot so that it crippled him, or caused some other such nefarious crime with her feet.

It so happened that this man wore false teeth—the glaringly white, obviously manufactured kind which to some persons are distasteful. Finally, goaded a bit beyond the ability to restrain herself, Susy said, "I don't think of myself as having such a bad problem. Frankly, I'd rather be lame than to have to wear false teeth."

Her opponent was startled to think that anyone could consider her plight in that favorable a light—or his plight that disagreeable. And this was just her point. While Susy thinks of being crippled as an opportunity to learn how kind people are to one with such a predicament and as an incentive to acquire more compassion for others with similar afflictions, this man thought of it only as punishment. And yet his false teeth to him were no punishment; they were merely a situation he had to endure.

I maintain that Susy Smith here missed an occasion for the perfect retort. She should have told this man that obviously in a past life he bit someone to death.

XVI
THE EXORCIST REVISITED

YOUR WORLD HAS recently been made widely conscious of the dangers of possession because of the book and moving picture called *The Exorcist* by William Peter Blatty. No, I have not seen the picture, but I am familiar with the sensation it has caused. I have learned of it vicariously when Susy read the novel, the movie reviews, and the newspaper accounts of scenes in theaters as viewers fainted or became sick with fright and revulsion.

Susy has also begun receiving letters asking for help, because it is becoming a fad to ascribe almost any mental discomfiture to evil spirits or demons. Reading the book or seeing the movie is such a harrowing experience that suggestible people find themselves identifying with the possessed little girl. Unfortunately it is probable that some of those who appeal for assistance may actually have a mischievous or even a malicious spirit intruding itself upon them; for such a situation as that described in the book is definitely factual on occasion.

While in the main seeming to attribute the possession to a demon, Blatty also raises the question of the possibility of spirit entities being involved as well. There is really no such supernatural entity as a demon or a devil, but there are evil men who act like the devil and think of themselves as demons. After they die they may be spirits of such malevolence that they can be called demons because of their vicious acts, not the least of which is possessing a mortal and causing him or her to do wild and unnatural things.

As you will recall, the child who is the protagonist of *The Exorcist* unwittingly invited the possessing entity by using the Ouija board with him. He soon became powerful enough that he got completely out of hand and moved into her body. This does not happen frequently to those who use Ouija boards or attempt automatic writing or other kinds of communication; but it *can* occur that a weak person is captured by a strong-willed evil-minded entity. This is why we continually advise against all efforts to communicate at random with spirits until you know how to protect yourself.

At the risk of being told that I am repeating myself, I feel it worthwhile to state once again the techniques I previously gave in the chapter on "Sex Between the Spheres." Before you make any attempts to communicate with spirits surround yourself with protection in order to keep intruders out and away. You must visualize yourself as completely wrapped in a powerful light of protection (often referred to as "the white Christ light"), and you must also state firmly that nothing can come near you that does not come from God in love and peace. If your visualization is persistent enough to be substantial and your statements are firm, they set up mental walls that can actually bar the unwanted interlopers. If you must attempt communication, always be alert to ascertain the true identity of the spirit who may be invisibly writing with you. You will recall that in 1 John 4:1 we are admonished: ". . . believe not every spirit, but try the spirits whether they are of God. . . ." If you should at any time suspect that those with whom you have managed to make contact are not pleasant, loving spirits, stop all efforts at communication immediately and order them out, firmly and vigorously. Give the formula for protection; and then . . . it would also be wise to appeal to the angels for assistance.

Of course, if you have a loved one who has died and wish to feel his presence or to assist his efforts to give you guardian angelship, that is entirely different, although you still have to be alert for evidence of identity. Just receiving the proper name should not convince you; you must have the feel of the person as well. If you loved someone who was malicious and hateful in life, however, do not attempt to contact him after his death. Pray for him instead.

Many instances of possession are going on throughout the world all the time. Primitive cultures know it for what it is, and they drive out the intruding entities with appropriate ceremonies to which he is likely to respond. Civilized people laugh at the idea of possession and either put the affected persons in mental institutions or subject them to long periods of psychotherapy, neither of which is likely to do much good.

If a priest is called in to exorcise such a demon, he may or may not achieve results. Sometimes, as in the book we are discussing, the clergyman may be laughed at and his ceremonies completely ignored by a demon who is in no way deterred by religious rituals. If, however, the evil entity had been influenced by Christianity when on earth, he would no doubt be impressed by the exorcism and might listen when it is applied against him. It may cause him to change for the better, or it may at least frighten him away from his obnoxious activity.

It is actually the rescue circles conducted by many mediums that do the most good for possession cases. Reform is made primarily by convincing these vicious men and women now in spirit form of the truth about their low states and the importance of changing their attitudes.

Not every case of possession is by a spirit so vile as to perform demonic acts. Many are merely indicative of a mischievous entity who obtains temporary possession of a weak-willed person and plays pranks for a time.

COMMENTARY:

An instance of possession by an entity who was not particularly mean and vicious but mostly just misguided is reported in Thirty Years Among the Dead. *It illustrates how what was perhaps the most effective rescue circle of all time operated. Dr. Carl Wickland, who was the head of a mental institution, discovered that his wife was a medium, and with her help he was able to remove a number of entities who were possessing some of his patients. When he published their case histories, he reported that the patients were given shock treatment to dislodge the spirit intruders. Then spirit helpers conducted the intruders from their victims into the entranced medium's body. They then spoke through her, told who they were and usually indicated that they were in a very disorganized mental state. Dr. Wickland talked to them, telling them what had actually happened to them, and instructed them not to return to the victim but to start their progression instead.*

One of Wickland's cases involves a little boy named Jack T. of Chicago who had been normal with a good disposition until the age of five, when he began to manifest precocious tendencies and act strangely. He fretted about things ordinarily foreign to a child's mind and acted in many ways like an adult, worrying over trifles, lying awake at night with strange mutterings and presentiments, and at times having an uncontrollable temper.

Jack was a boy of nice appearance but now he talked constantly of being old and ugly looking, and he was so intractable that efforts to reprimand and correct him proved of no avail. This condition became so aggravated that his family despaired of Jack's reason, and so they asked Dr. Wickland for help. Then a spirit whose actions and expressions were in every way like those the boy had recently been exhibiting spoke through Mrs. Wickland and explained his situation.

"This entity," writes Wickland, "said his name was Charlie Herrmann; he was aware of having died and declared that he was a very homely man, with ugly features and a face covered with pockmarks. Nobody had cared for him and this fact preyed on his mind.

"Someone had once told him that after death individuals could reincarnate and become whatever they wished to be. Since his only desire was to be good looking, so that others would not shun him, he decided to try and reincarnate.

"As a result, he became entangled in the magnetic aura of a small boy and was unable to free himself."

Finding that he was helplessly imprisoned and incapable of making anyone realize it, Charlie Herrmann had outbursts of temper and "felt like flying to pieces," he said.

They called him Jack and he didn't like it. He had been miserable while attached to the child but could do nothing about it. Through the help he received from the Wicklands, he was freed, and very grateful; and Jack became the good and happy boy he had previously been. I hope the spirits who took Charlie off to help him taught him right away how to think himself handsome.

There are also instances where a spirit not deliberately intending to cause harm moves in on someone for a specific purpose and takes over the use of his body temporarily. This happens frequently when drunks pass out and then revive with all the characteristics of someone else. It *is* someone else—a spirit craving the taste of liquor—who usurps his body. After death one who has long dominated someone who is weak and insipid may continue to do so invisibly, even to the extent of possessing him. There are occasions when the owner of the body fights back when attacked by a spirit who tries to take him over. Sometimes the two consciousnesses may alternate in control of the body. There are cases diagnosed as hysteria, dissociation or schizophrenia that are actually attributable to exactly this.

Obsession is similar to possession, except that it is intermittent instead of continuous. It is more of an overshadowing or influencing of the thoughts of the victim than a complete takeover.

Occasionally a spirit may momentarily overshadow someone highly sensitive or psychic and impress his thoughts on this person. If they are reflections about something that has occurred in the past, and if the sensitive knows anything about the theory of reincarnation, he will usually attribute what he believes to be his own fleeting memories to evidence of a past life.

COMMENTARY:

In Your Mysterious Powers of ESP, Harold Sherman reports an instance of a childhood psychic adventure about which Mrs. Dessie L. of Long Beach, California, wrote him. She believes it proves reincarnation, but Sherman has another explanation for it.

When Dessie was a child she was on a camping trip with her father and her brother George. They came to a spot where none of them had ever been before, where a house had once stood in a leafy vale. Dessie began to have a battle with herself because she felt impelled to run down the hill. When she did and her father reproved her, she told him, "My dishes were hidden down there" and "My swing was just under the hill." After some argument that she couldn't possibly be aware of what was in such a completely unknown area, her father and brother went with her down the hill.

She then showed them a tree with the remains of a swing on it, and they dug in the earth where she indicated and found what she described in advance as "Haviland china, white with blue decorations." Her father buried the dishes again, oddly enough, for he knew the girl's mother would never understand. (I'd have told her they found a present for her in a secondhand store. Wouldn't a little white lie have been justified on such an occasion?)

Dessie concluded her letter to Harold, "I don't know what you will think of this, but to my mind, at least, it is a very sacred story, and proof positive of reincarnation."

Why should the woman think it had to be herself in a past life who hid those dishes? Because that is the only explanation she knew. Sherman had a better one: "To me, it is not proof of reincarnation—it is evidence of possession by a discarnate entity, by one of the persons who lived in the old house that was now rotted away, who had remained there, earthbound, for years with his or her attention and feelings fixed on an emotional moment when it was necessary to hide the prized dishes to keep them, possibly, from being stolen by vandals of some sort.

"For the first time, perhaps, in all the years since this person had died, a sensitive individual had chanced on the scene—young Dessie, whose entire life history gives evidence of her unusual psychic gifts. Up until that moment, when she testified that she began having a battle with herself (probably the attempt of the discarnate entity to take possession) she had never had a thought about another life. She had not the slightest feeling that this was anything but a lovely, shady spot for a campsite.... Of course, she would feel that they were her dishes under the influence of this possessive spirit, acting through her, so that the two were temporarily of one mind."

Sherman adds by way of explanation that he has had personal experiences in taking on the environmental conditions of similar places, sensing conditions and activities and even personalities that formerly existed there. He knows how real this can feel, especially to such a highly sensitized, impressionable child as Dessie was at the time. "She would certainly not be in any position to analyze—only to react, to feel deeply, as the entity felt during the period of possession," he says.

"The influence that caused Dessie to feel as she did, to know and to act, was gone as quickly as it had come, once she departed from the premises," writes Sherman. "Another psychic, taken into this area, might have walked into the same situation and produced additional verifiable impressions. It is difficult to arrange a follow-up investigation of spontaneous cases of this kind."

Many mediums have had the experience of seeing a spirit overshadow someone and influence his thoughts. There are some sensitives who will never go into bars under any circumstances because they can see, around many of the drinkers, spirits attempting to experience vicariously the taste of alcohol. If such an entity finds one who overdrinks to the point of insensibility, he may quite possibly occupy the body, bring it back to consciousness and have a great many more drinks before he too loses it to insensibility.

Mediums have a large place in life and could do a tremendous amount of good if they would use their ability to see spirits as an opportunity to convert the degenerates from their earthbound ways. They should always do whatever they can to talk to them and explain their condition to them. As I have previously mentioned, because such a spirit's mind is closely concentrated on earth, he will listen to someone in the flesh more readily than he will listen to those of us who are disembodied. And so a medium should always start talking to the unenlightened at any time that he sees one or senses his presence. I believe the time will come when sensitives will feel this to be one of the obligations imposed upon them by their unusual talents. Theirs is a great endowment, and not one to be taken lightly.

Mediums would be of special value to doctors who work with mental patients, if they were employed. But with medical understanding such as it is today, it seldom happens that intruding spirits are recognized and eliminated. When a psychiatrist or psychologist is able to bring himself to use the services of a psychic, he finds that many of his patients are revealed to have earthbound entities intruding themselves upon them.

COMMENTARY:

In Widespread Psychic Wonders *(Ace, 1970) I described an experience told me by my friend, the late New York City psychologist, neurologist and psychical researcher Dr. Russell MacRobert. It involved a patient of his and the medium Frank Decker. In the years before they both died the doctor and the medium had developed a mutually advantageous arrangement whereby Decker occasionally assisted with suggestions about a particular patient. An example of how the services of a medium can be of value to a psychiatrist oc-*

curred on a day when Decker dropped by the doctor's Park Avenue office and waited until MacRobert had time to see him. A young man also sitting in the waiting room particularly interested the medium and he watched him carefully. After this patient had gone into Dr. MacRobert's private office, had had his appointment and then left, Frank Decker went in. He asked immediately, "Who is that young man who just left?"

"Why?" countered the doctor, sure that something interesting was coming.

"Because he has a real bad problem," said Decker. "There's a dirty old man with him, hanging around him so closely that he is almost overshadowing the young man's personality."

"What does he look like?" MacRobert asked. He well knew the technique of interviewing mediums without giving anything away, yet at the same time showing interest and curiosity about the message to come.

Decker described the entity he had observed. "Well, he's toothless, and he's very unenlightened. He does not know he is dead. He seems to be clinging to the young man as one in a dream, not really knowing what is going on."

Dr. MacRobert later told me how helpful this information was in his analysis of the patient. "That boy," he said, "was less than thirty but he had a strange fixation about being old. It was all I could do to convince him that he should not go and have all his teeth pulled out. He thought of himself as prematurely aging, tired, ill, and with decayed teeth—although anyone who looked at him could see that he was in excellent shape . . . and so were his teeth. I'd had great difficulty with him, not knowing just what his actual problem was. When Decker saw the toothless old man possessing, or at least obsessing, him, I knew what to do."

There are cases, more frequently from India, in which certain children begin at the age of three or four, perhaps, to tell stories about things they say happened to them long before. As they grow older, if they are taken to the locale where they claim these incidents occurred, they sometimes can identify people and places they would have no normal means of recognizing. It is thought by their parents and friends that they are identifying scenes from a former lifetime. The truth is that such instances represent strong cases of spirit influence, or even sometimes possibly of possession.

Shanti Devi, for instance, is a lady of Delhi, India, who is well known in the West because her case has been written up so many times as an instance of past-life recall. It is obvious to me that when she was a child, she was strongly influenced by a spirit. The records reveal that this was the spirit of a young woman named Lugdi who had died in childbirth in the nearby town of Muttra. Believing it possible to come back in another body, and not wanting to leave her newborn son, Lugdi entered or overshadowed a baby born a few years later—Shanti Devi, who began to speak of her past life almost as soon as she was able to talk. By the time she was nine years old, Shanti was so insistent that she be taken to visit her husband in Muttra that her parents complied with her wishes. There she identified Lugdi's husband, her son, and other persons and places in what could only be called a supernormal manner, for Shanti Devi had never before been to the city of Muttra. As the girl grew older the memories of the prior life were spoken of less and less, probably because the spirit of Lugdi had withdrawn her attention from Shanti.

COMMENTARY:

A very good instance of past-life recall that illustrates James' point of spirit influence is the case of Jasbir, which is reported by Dr. Ian Stevenson in Twenty Cases Suggestive of Reincarnation *as a case of possession, which it obviously is.*

Jasbir was a boy who died of smallpox in the spring of 1954 at the age of three and a half. He was to be buried the next morning; but sometime during the night his body stirred and came back to life. Within a few weeks he was well enough to talk, and then it was revealed that his personality and character had changed entirely. He was now speaking in a Brahmin dialect, and insisted he was someone else altogether, a higher-caste Brahmin.

Jasbir maintained now that he was Sobha Ram of Vehedi, a nearby village. As he grew older he reported many instances in the life of Sobha Ram which were later confirmed, telling how he met his death at the age of twenty-two during a wedding celebration when he had fallen off a chariot and been killed. The details the boy told about Sobha Ram's life and death were proved to have been factual, and when he finally was taken to Vehedi, he knew the way to Sobha Ram's home and recognized all the people that young man had known. He was only happy when in Vehedi, and so arrangements were made that he could spend most of his summers with the family he claimed to have been his own in his past life.

Dr. Stevenson said he had interviewed all the people concerned in this case and believed that they were telling the truth. It is very clearly a case of possession in which the deceased man took over the body just vacated by the spirit of the boy. His psychic force was strong enough to enable the body to return to life and usefulness, and he remained in it from then on.

One of the worst features of taking drugs is that it lays one open to the possibility of obsession or possession. When you lose control of your mind on any kind of drug and throw it wide open to what you hope will be fascinating new sensations and visions, you are also opening it to intruding entities. If you allow them to influence you by taking the drugs often, you may soon find that you are completely unable to control your mind yourself.

For a malicious earthbound spirit to try deliberately to take over another's mind is a vicious thing, but it is done frequently to those who overindulge in either alcohol or narcotics. Being aware of the possibility will help you to keep it from happening to you. Stay away from all other mind-influencing drugs as carefully as you stay away from heroin. If you wish to have happy visions, think happy thoughts so frequently that they become a habit. Then learn the proper system of meditation and the pleasant pictures will come without any outside stimulation causing them. And you will not be in danger of the unfortunate consequences of spirit intrusion.

One of the worst things that has to be faced when you finally become aware of the possibility of spirit influence is that some of it is harmful. I do not like to have to be the one to bring you bad news, but if I am to present the entire picture of life after death I have to reveal to you that there is a strata of unprincipled spirits that is very close to your earth and is doing it inconceivable damage. It is good for you to be aware of this so that you can be protected against it. Ignoring its existence and pretending it will go away will not solve the problem. The only way truly to do that is to clean up your world to the extent that there are not many evil men dying. That is a long, slow process, but it is the hope of the future.

In the meantime persons who are aware of the danger of possession are not the ones who become possessed . . . if they know enough to protect themselves.

XVII

MEDIUMS ARE A NECESSITY

To be able to find a good medium of communication is a wonderful thing for us. So many on this side are eager to get the word about life after death through to the world, and they are one of our few means of doing it.

Some people, of course, are psychic enough themselves that they are able to receive messages from their departed friends. These may come as hunches, words of warning, admonition or encouragement, or visions. Many poets, artists, musicians and other artistic people are quite psychic. Their sensitivity makes them good at their crafts, and it also allows them to be aided by spirits. You are no doubt familiar with many incidents in which authors have admitted to awareness that the plots for their stories have come automatically into their minds without their thinking processes being involved. They know what mediums know, that it is easy to distinguish what comes from their own cerebration and what is superimposed on their minds from outside. Many poets know this also. Others have enjoyed the assistance of spirits and angels without being aware of it.

Dreaming is a good means of contact between the spheres. Many of your dreams are messages to you from your own subconscious mind, if you can but interpret them. But other dreams may be thoughts implanted in your mind by spirits while you are asleep.

Nightly visits during sleep are often quite successful as well. A dreamer in a very deep sleep may have an out-of-the-body experience and visit with his relatives and friends over here. He may not remember more than a snatch or two of this when he awakens, or he may remember the whole thing. Some most inspirational experiences occur this way.

In deep meditation one may have a meeting of minds with spirit friends. Some persons have been able to sit, as Susy is sitting now, at a typewriter or a desk with pen or pencil in hand and produce automatic writing. This has brought a lot of information from us over the years, as has the Ouija board on occasion, and even the pendulum or a rapping table. If you are not familiar with some of the evidential material that has been received in such manner, you must read *Life is Forever* by Susy Smith (G. P. Putnam's Sons, 1974). It is a book full of evidence, which this present work does not attempt to be.

The medium who has developed his or her psychic sensitivity to a high degree is the best possible means of communication, however, and the one to whom we must look for some of the best evidence achievable. I could only wish there were more good mediums today. It is too easy for an individual who has some slight psychic ability to make reputation and money by occasional minor feats of clairvoyance or telepathy or precognition or healing, and so very few will go to the trouble to develop so that their capacities are really top-notch.

Going into trance is almost a lost art because it is too much trouble to learn and too much discomfort to endure, and so even those who could develop powerful mediumship of this sort do not bother. Many of the greatest trance mediums have disliked that technique immensely, and it is hard to blame them, for they have missed all the enjoyment of their séances. When asleep, they have been unable to participate in the activities, and have learned about what occurred only when they came out of trance.

Since it is possible for us to get accurate messages through a medium who is mildly entranced, this is what we wish to encourage among you psychic folk today, if you will only develop to that point and then make yourselves available to us. Many could train themselves to be sensitives if they would make the effort. When the time comes that psychic ability is looked on as a great talent and mediums are taken seriously by the general public, then more people will be agreeable to spending the time and effort to develop.

I am not particularly recommending professional mediumship, for talents fluctuate, and if one is making his living by his psychic abilities and is incapable of performing on occasion, it puts him in a spot. If he is unable to produce genuine phenomena or messages, he should be obligated to return the sitter's money; yet if his livelihood depends on it, he is too often tempted to fill in with the fruits of his imagination . . . or even, in some cases . . . fraud.

The solution to this problem—except for subsidization of mediums by government agencies or wealthy persons—is for home circles once again to become popular, as they were briefly around the time of the First World War. If more groups were sitting for development of their psychic abilities, soon a whole generation of mediums would be available for our use. We have so much to give you, if you will only perfect the means whereby we may be able to do so. What we want to tell you people through mediums is not what stocks to buy or which horse will win at the races or even whether or not you should take certain steps. We do not want to run your lives for you, even though on occasion we are able to help out with judicious suggestions. No, our main goal is to give you proof of life after death.

It is an unfortunate fact that without genuine personal growth on the medium's part, one can never be sure of the rendering of wisdom that comes through his mind. It may be true, or it may be polluted by his personal desire, pride or false reasoning. Some professional mediums have given the whole subject of spirit communication a bad name. It is therefore difficult for most lay people to accept the reality of genuine mediumship and understand its value. When each home has its own private sensitive, then all will be different. The ordinary household variety of psychic could exist among many family or neighborhood groups, with circles that meet regularly for development of the members. Then new mediums would constantly be available, and contact would be facilitated between our planes and yours.

It may not be easy at first to find a meditation group or development class with which to sit. Sometimes the only solution is to start your own among your friends. You will all grow spiritually as you sit together, even though you may not see results of a psychical nature for quite a while. Do not be discouraged. As time goes on one or more of you may develop more rapidly than the others, and then his or her talents will assist the others to develop, because psychic talent always tends to increase in proportion to the achievements of any one of the group.

When people sit together to meditate and develop, many interested spirits immediately gather to give their assistance. We bring you great measures of love, and we are willing to work endlessly for your advancement. You will all feel this loving warmth to the point that you will come to look forward to your weekly class night with great anticipation.

If you meet for the right purposes and know how to protect yourselves, your safety is assured, so do not worry. In your development circles you are opening up your centers of awareness on several levels. For this reason, during the time that you are making yourselves receptive to spirit influence you must be sure that you are determined to live honestly, earnestly and sincerely. If you maintain self-discipline and keep yourselves on a plane of integrity, purity of motive, and good common sense, with a strong element of humor, your experiences are bound to be pleasant and successful. Earthbound spirits hate happy, well-adjusted people, and they will have nothing to do with you, so your group will be perfectly safe if you follow the techniques I have set down in this book.

COMMENTARY:

The James-Underhill material expands on this as follows:

"In the early stages of development you become extremely sensitive. It is essential that you should be able to create a psychic sheath through which no undesirable influence can penetrate. Visualize around yourself a transparent, iridescent wall, something like a soap bubble, at arm's length from your body. Think frequently of that sheath until you succeed in feeling it around you and know that it is strong and elastic in texture. Think of it confidently as a reality, for it can become a very strong one. It is created out of actual invisible matter, which is a substance that may be manipulated by means of thought. Know that all beneficent influences can find access to you through this shell or sheath, but that no evil or disintegrating forces can reach you. Make a habit of working on this protective wall until you feel quite secure from harm. But remember that in order to maintain it intact, you must not entertain the

type of thought that would attract evil to you. Fear also weakens your psychic sheath. Doubt about the efficacy of your shield robs it of its power of resistance. However, you may be certain that if you work with a positive mind in creating this shell and maintaining it, you will succeed in rendering yourself immune from outer attacks.

"*If you ever have any reason to suspect that you are being psychically attacked, keep a light burning by your bedside during the night.*"

Always begin all your meetings with a prayer and keep a prayerful attitude during them. If anyone who does not like to do this or who in any way has an irritating effect on the members of your circle asks to join your group discourage him from coming. Your mutual rapport is one of the things that will make the evenings you set aside for development among the happiest times of your life.

The technique that I would suggest for attempting to attain a mildly trancelike state (in which you will be receptive to the thought vibrations we helpful spirit associates will set in motion) is this: It will not be necessary for you to go to sleep during the half hour or forty-five minutes your group sits quietly in semidarkness. Rather, you might seek a state of mental withdrawal, which might best be accomplished by trying a form of self-hypnosis.

Never attempt this when alone, but only when you are with a group, the best size of which is anywhere from five to ten people. After prayers have been said and the lights dimmed and each of you has mentally stated your protection, say to yourself that you are withdrawing your consciousness into a sleeplike state so that you can be used for communication with enlightened spirits, and then put yourself into our hands. When thoughts run through your mind, as they constantly will, attempt to distract yourself from them by repeating slowly and quietly in your mind that you are going deeper and deeper into a trancelike state. There is no reason to fear that you will go to sleep in any way that will be harmful to you if you are in a circle of people who have surrounded themselves with protection—and if you personally have done the same thing. Do not ever do this when you are alone.

Even though you will be telling yourself to sleep, there is little likelihood that you will ever go into a deep trance until the time comes that you are thoroughly under the control of wise spirit guides. When you are in a development group, you are in our hands, and we will take care of you. So you need have no fear.

If you should happen to go to sleep, members of your circle can bring you out of it gently when the quiet time is over. Usually you will just go into a mildly trancelike state that will be useful to us. If we should begin to speak through you during this time, try not to listen to what is being said. Others will tell you later what it was. Just keep saying inwardly, "Deeper and deeper into trance. I am asleep. I am not thinking about what is going on. I am sleeping, sleeping, deeper and deeper asleep."

Perhaps your particular forte will not be trance mediumship, but clairvoyance, and you may begin to see pictures or lights. During the quiet period it is not a good practice for different members of the group to speak out or tell what they are seeing or hearing or getting telepathically. They should remember it until afterward, or if this is difficult, they should bring with them a notebook and pencil and write down what comes to them in the dark. When everyone compares notes later, the numerous parallels that occur are often quite interesting.

Remember that training one or two of your group as semitrance mediums is the most important endeavor of your evenings, and so do not be distracted if they speak out. But if everyone else is talking all through the meeting, then no one will have enough quiet to develop anything. I know that many mediums and many circles prefer to allow everyone to speak aloud at any time they see, hear, or feel anything during the evening. Some mediums have trained this way, but on the whole it is most distracting and is not a good technique to employ.

Many people who believe themselves to be psychic wish to develop and do not know how. You may not soon find a group with which to sit or friends who want to join you in starting one. Do not fret. The time will come when you will, if you don't mind waiting.

I cannot say that any of this will be easy; it takes a great deal of patience and discipline. Even after you have found a group and begun to sit, you may discover that you are very slow to develop while others may be faster. Those who back up the growth of a medium are just as valuable as he is, and your psychic power may be more useful for the assistance of others. If this occurs, try not to be disappointed. Each of you has a valuable place to fill where you can be helpful.

Remember that you will all have the loving attention of many of us in the spirit world who will work with you when the time comes for your development, or your assistance in the development of others. Just do not be precipitate and attempt to communicate with spirits alone. When all is ready, assemblies of good spirits will get together with you and any group of responsible persons you can find who will sit one night every week. Send your thoughts of love to them, and they in turn will send theirs to you. I hope they will someday bring through you messages that will inspire the people of the world to know their immortality.

XVIII

CHILDREN ARE TO BE CHERISHED

RAISING A CHILD properly in today's complicated world is an extremely difficult undertaking. It will demand all the discipline parents can acquire in order to give their offspring a proper foundation so that he can cope with existence.

If all life on your planet were peaceful and serene, there would be less for you to do to raise your child properly; but it would also be less of a challenge to you. And challenges are what you thrive on. So when you decide to have a baby, face the fact that it won't be easy, and guide yourself accordingly.

If all of you on earth can learn proper procedures and follow them, all life will alter for the better quite soon, and conditions for your descendants will be immeasurably improved. But "all of you" actually means each individual one of you. You, yourself, must make the effort. It will therefore be your personal plan to try to make your child an example for others, and the secret of that is to make his earliest days as secure as possible. This is done by loving him so thoroughly and devoting yourself to him so completely that his first years give him nothing but peace and inner serenity. No matter what poor environment a baby is born into, if both his mother and his father love him and teach him to love others and to think constructively, he will not have all the character problems his playmates have. He will live relatively free of those insecurities that plague others.

No, I am not overlooking much of what makes up a lifetime—the harassments, the unhappiness, the adjustments one constantly has to make in order merely to endure his existence. Of course you and your child will have difficulties. No life is so rosy that it can be without irritations, exasperations, humiliations, and even some genuine misery. How else can you learn? Even utopia will not be carefree, when the time comes that it is finally achieved. There is no reason for anyone to expect that it will ever be possible for man to sail through life without the striving, the effort, and the pressures that produce character. To anticipate growing without seasoning is ridiculous; but if you have a good start, you can overcome everything.

Let me put it this way: Your character is developed according to the pressures you function against. To illustrate this point, the son of wealthy socialites who has three divorced wives and five or six children scattered about, whom he either neglects completely or grudgingly supports but to whom he never allocates any of his time and attention, can be contrasted to a particular African pygmy in most primitive circumstances. This native loves his children well, gives them a thorough grounding in how to live in the wilderness, and spends many weary hours every day hunting or digging for roots in order to find food for his family. His pressures are greater in every way, but he learns from them and will be much farther ahead spiritually when he dies than the other man. If the pygmy has more to master educationally and culturally in the spirit world, the rich blue blood has much more to learn about love and compassion.

Ideally every child would come into the world with a heritage of a strong physical body and good mental capabilities, and he would be raised with love and understanding in pleasant surroundings. This ideal is destined someday to be realized on earth, but I would hate to say how long away that time is. Until then, each individual has to progress as best he can with the abilities he has in the situations in which he finds himself. This does not mean that those who are handicapped or poor are deliberately discriminated against by God. Neither does it mean that they are making karmic retribution for crimes committed in previous lives.

It is his use of the capacities with which he was born that makes a man of character; it does not matter what specific problems he has to overcome as he develops. If you were born blind, it is the effect of causes put into motion before your birth. Perhaps your mother had a disease or an accident while carrying you, which resulted in your blindness. There is no reason to bemoan the fate of the poor individual without sight. Granted that it makes his life on earth more difficult; it is how he accepts it that is important. And after he has gone that first mile—his earth life—in the dark, his eyes will be joyously opened for the rest of his trip through his eternal existence. Each individual has many challenges to meet during his life. If he meets them well when blind—and there are many happy and fulfilled sightless people in the world—he will progress faster than someone who may have started his life with a perfect body yet has done very little with his capabilities. If you are crippled, it is because certain causes occurred—you may have fallen down and badly injured yourself, or you may have had poliomyelitis, or you might have been in an automobile accident or have a war injury. But whatever the cause, whatever the effect, enduring with fortitude builds character. Others who have no such handicap as you do may make less of their opportunities.

Maladjustments in life may be emotional as well as physical. A wealthy child would be said to have a good karma because he has a beautiful healthy body, a lovely home, and all kinds of toys to play with. He may nonetheless be unwanted and unloved and life for him may be much less rewarding than it is for some who are poor and handicapped.

No matter how difficult it is for you, raising your child wisely, with love and intelligence, and making a well-adjusted adult of him is one of the greatest contributions you can make to the human race. Disciplined parents who set an example by never speaking disparagingly of others, or rudely to them—who raise happy children in harmonious surroundings—are themselves happy, however, so they do not need to feel that they are sacrificing if they attempt always to keep their homes free of discord.

If a husband and wife cannot be contented with each other, they should be intelligent enough not to have children in the first place. When you consider acquiring a family, think of the detailed amount of time and effort you will have to spend to raise it properly. If you do not feel equal to such a big expenditure of effort, do not even let yourself consider the project. Do not plan to have a family until you are sure that you, yourself, and your spouse are mentally and emotionally mature. If this sounds as if I am trying to reduce the population of the world, why not? Overpopulation is a problem, and babies should not be brought into a world that cannot care for them properly.

You should never have a child just because he will be an adorable little extension of your own ego, to be cuddled while he is small and cute, scolded when he grows older and misbehaves, and then left to his own resources to develop into an ill-adjusted human being with the problems of adapting himself to existence. This has consistently been the custom of the world, but that does not make it right. If you are not able to raise children under the best possible conditions, then do not give birth to them. And do not feel guilty if you choose not to have any. Be proud of making a sensible choice.

Throughout this book you will notice that I am talking to you as if you were responsible individuals with free will to accomplish what you wish with your character and personality. This is because you are just that. All the alibiing in the world about your childhood traumas, et cetera, will not relieve you of one iota of accountability for what you ultimately become. When you face up to this and realize the difficulties you are having (because of the way you were raised and because of all the negative patterns programmed into you, which you later have to unlearn in order to be successful as a person), can you not see why I demand of you proper consideration for your children so that their lives will be proportionately easier than yours have been?

Youngsters who marry because of pregnancy and then raise an unwanted and unloved child are not just pathetic. They are unthinking and unkind. Today there are prescriptions that make it possible not to have unwanted babies. In a culture (many of whose mores I do not condone) where young people are frequently thrown together alone in intimate circumstances before they have learned to control their passions, facing facts and being prepared for eventualities is an indication of intelligent forethought, not unrestraint.

Philandering husbands, or wives, married couples who cannot get along and think having a baby might bring them into a better relationship, and those who observe that new social custom of yours of living together openly and having children out of wedlock—none of these may be delighted with what I have to say about this, for I suggest that you either observe the proprieties and stay home and take care of your young or else do not have any. Unless you are able to change your habits for your child and can love him despite what you have to give up for him, then do not bear him in the first place. There is no compromise. Of course, if you already have very young children and feel that you have to leave them to go to work—not to support them, which is very commendable—but in order to give them, and yourself, luxuries, I am talking to you, too.

COMMENTARY:
  It is interesting how the world catches up with James. This bold statement about children was received from him in 1967 and was published in 1971 in my book Confessions of a Psychic. In Time, December 24, 1973, the following appeared:
  "Ironically, the exodus of mothers from the home coincides with a spate of new studies on the importance of the first few months and years of childhood. The most important of these is an unfinished trilogy by British psychoanalyst John Bowlby, who has devoted most of his life and over eight hundred pages to demonstrating the need for little children to have a consistent mother figure. 'Formerly, adolescence was thought to be the most critical age; the very early years are now being recognized as such,' says Jane Judge, director of Sarah Lawrence College's Early Childhood Center. Can day-care centers serve babies well? The debate rages."

  Although I am firm about your not giving birth to children unless you can provide them with the specifics I know are important, there is a loophole for you if you ardently desire to expend your love on a child . . . a most worthwhile motive. If you feel unfulfilled without a baby, but find that other conditions are not right for you to have one of your own, then adopt one of the many who need any kind of help desperately. If you can. I understand they are making it more and more difficult to do this. Perhaps you could get a war orphan from another country. If nothing else, you can send money to a war-torn country to aid orphans who are raised by funding from America. Take out your parental affection by helping these poor little waifs and you will be doing them, yourself, and the world a good turn.
  As far as the ideal conditions in which to raise a child, they are

quite demanding. From the time the small one arrives until he is at least seven or eight years old, the parents should consider their own lives secondary to his. If this sounds impossible, stop and think what you are undertaking. You are giving personal identity to and raising an individual who will live forever. He has a great deal to offer the world if he learns to adjust adequately to life. He will be unable to do this successfully unless you provide him with a firm foundation of character. Parents who have children needlessly, carelessly, and without considering the cost to the offspring of inadequate heritage and training, who bring unwanted infants into the world without preparing themselves to give them loving care, are criminals! I do not say this lightly. They are perpetrating crimes just as surely as if they robbed or murdered. A personality that has been stunted because of improper upbringing is a life that should not have been started in the first place. Do you want to be responsible for the production of an earthbound spirit?

I am willing to go out on a limb about this and make statements you may find even more difficult to accept than what I have already said. In his earliest years a child should not be allowed to play with others who might have a bad influence on him; and if you cannot keep unpleasant neighbor children away from him, you should move. It is more important for the young to have proper associates than for adults. If your environment is wrong for your child and if those with whom he plays are rude, impolite, undisciplined or vulgar, by all means keep him away from them even if you have to move from the neighborhood to do it. Do not scoff at this. Do not say, "His father's business is here and making a good living for the family is the most important thing." It is not. A child does not absolutely have to be well-dressed or have anything but the basic necessities to eat. He does not need piano lessons or dancing classes or any luxuries. He can work his way through college or get a scholarship if you have not acquired the money to send him by the time he is ready for it. But he does have to have agreeable surroundings in his earliest years, pleasant associates, constructive thoughts, and much, much love.

My last suggestion to parents is to begin telling your child about his spirit helpers at an early age and train him in positive thinking. Don't forget the aphorism I told you to teach him to start his days with: "Today I will be healthy and happy all day long." Let him know not only that there is a God in heaven but that there are angels who love him and want to help him, even though he cannot see them. Suggest to him that he probably has a guardian angel of his very own. If this rapport with his invisible friends is established in his youth, many of his biggest problems in life will be solved with their able assistance, and it will be possible for him to avoid some of the mishaps that could occur to him without the benefit of their farseeing viewpoint. I know I said you need pressures in order to build character; but you do not need too many of them, and anything that will make life easier should be accepted gladly.

If you begin to suspect that your child is naturally psychic, by all means encourage him. The psychic child may be extremely sensitive and open to misunderstanding, so tell him it is quite natural that he can see what you cannot, and ask him to describe his invisible playmates to you if he has them. It would be thoughtful of you not to sit on a chair if he says the unseen little Tommy is sitting there. In other words, respect his differences from the norm in this regard. Psychic ability is a truly great potentiality and should be encouraged just as much as any other abilities would be.

When certain talents have been inherited and a child has definite tendencies in any specific area, whether it be psychic, music, art, or mathematics, then spirits with similar interests take him in their charge and become guardian angels to him. Thus, he has especially gifted invisible assistants as he grows up. They encourage his talents and this puts him so much ahead of others in his particular line that he is often considered a genius.

COMMENTARY:
There is a published account revealing just how this has worked in the life of a modern violinist. Florizel von Reuter, eighty-two-year-old American violinist and composer, conductor and music teacher, was a violin prodigy because before his birth his mother wanted more than anything for him to become a famous musician. The name best known to her was Nicolo Paganini (1782–1840), and so she implored his spirit to guide her unborn baby, beseeching him night and day for his influence. When the child was born, she dedicated him to the ideal for which she had striven. Florizel accepted the responsibility from his earliest youth, amazing his teachers not only with his skill but also with his feats of memory. He often

spoke of someone who was with him when he practiced. "Some old master is always listening," he would comment. "I mustn't disappoint him."

Von Reuter said in his book Psychical Experiences of a Musician that it was not until he was thirty that he began his search for survival evidence. One of his first spirit communicators was Paganini, who spoke at a voice sitting. Florizel was told: "There is a great violinist present who wants to greet the young man. He says his name is Paganini." Then the spirit of the old violinist, purporting to speak through the medium, thanked Florizel's mother for having influenced him to become interested in the child and his music.

Mrs. von Reuter, also present at the séance, said, "Florizel plays all your twenty-four caprices."

"I know," was the answer. "I have often been present in concerts where he has performed them."

Florizel von Reuter says he doesn't doubt it for a moment. Sometimes when he has been playing the violin he has felt his hands moved to a better fingering than the one he had in mind, and he knew it was Paganini helping him.

Do your best to see that your psychic child is schooled in the areas in which his special abilities lie, for he is often creative and a means of expression is vitally necessary to his or her well-being. Above all, never let him feel that you consider him odd. Foster the growth of healthy roots and you will see fine results in later years.

Be sure, however, that your child is warned not to talk to his playmates about his guardian angels or, if he is psychic enough to have them, his invisible playmates. They should be as personal and as little discussed as his other private habits.

Susy suggests that a child raised to know only love and compassion and guardian angels will be "absolutely clobbered when he gets with those little monsters in school!"

I hope he will not. By the time he is of school age he should be warned that his new associates have not been taught all the wonderful things he knows and that he must not worry if they do not understand. He should feel sorry for them instead. Then, with his inbred warmth and loving personality and serenity of spirit he will probably win over even the most arrogant, although he will be self-sufficient enough to be happy without their approval if he should not gain it. Do not anticipate any additional troubles for this individual who has been indoctrinated correctly since infancy. His life will be an example for all to follow. He will have his share of unhappiness, unforseen developments of one kind or another, deaths in his family and the like, but his backlog of personal security and harmony will carry him through anything.

If you and your spouse do not care to live your private lives with wisdom, that is your business. But if you take on the responsibility of giving birth, then it becomes someone else's business . . . and this someone—your child—should be the most important person in the world to you. He demands and must have the very best that is in you at all times. If you do not provide him with affection and wise attention, you are neglecting your duty, no matter how well you feed, house, and clothe him and how much money you spend on him. Money, I need not tell you, makes life more comfortable and easier to bear, but it does not provide character. That you must acquire for yourself through strenuous effort.

The wonderful thing about it is that when you exert yourself wisely for love of someone else, your own character develops without your even being aware of it.

XIX
ANIMALS ARE FOREVER

LIFE FORCE COMES from Ultimate Perfection, and it goes on eternally. Only the consciousnesses of human beings return to become a component of the Divine, however.

The animating spirit of life comes directly from Supreme Intelligence into each living thing, which always continues to exist in its spiritual counterpart after the death or disintegration of the matter in which it was encased on earth. In animals, plants or humans, the spiritual essence remains constant whether with or without a physical body. For this reason the Astral in its higher aspects looks exactly like your world, for it has a duplicate of all the living things of the earth. When an animal is killed or dies, it does not know it, for its awareness continues to exist in its spirit body exactly as it always has.

Consciousnesses never arrive in a human being after progressing upward from the lower animals. There is no such thing as transmigration of souls either up or down the intellectual scale. No human infant has ever received a consciousness that had formerly lived as any other aspect of life, either plant or animal, and no man is ever sent back to live a life as an animal. There have been occasions, though, when deceased persons who believed they must transmigrate and inhabit a beast as a form of punishment or retribution have actually possessed some animals for a period of time.

COMMENTARY:

An extremely bizarre experience, reported to me by Mrs. Yvonne Odell of Miami, Florida, might be offered as a possible verification of this statement by James. Yvonne, who has been psychic all her life, is the only person I know of, with the possible exception of the fictional Dr. Doolittle, who ever listened to an elephant talk.

"On Christmas Day, 1959," *she told me*, "my husband and I were enjoying a visit to the Crandon Park Zoo. Tiring of watching the monkeys with John, I wandered alone to a deserted place where a lone elephant was chained. She was a female named Elsie who has since died. As I stood there observing her monotonously swinging back and forth, waving her trunk and flapping her ears, I thought, 'Poor thing, what a life.'

"Now, for a long time I have experimented successfully with telepathy and clairvoyance. [*She was tested for years by the now defunct Florida Society for Psychical Research.*] Although I fail at sending messages, I am able to receive them. Whenever this happens, something like an electric shock of vibrations goes through my entire body. I seem to be temporarily paralyzed, although my mind remains perfectly conscious and alert. While I was standing there thinking about the sad lot of being an elephant, suddenly the familiar shock of vibrations ran through my body. I was getting a message from the elephant! It was not in words, but in impressions. I could see a famous figure of history who had murdered many people, and I became aware that this man's mind was now captured within the elephant. I was glued to the spot and could not move one inch. Clairvoyantly I saw crowds, chariots, I heard weird music, trumpets, shouts, horrible noises; and then I saw the arena with martyred Christians screaming in agony. I thought I would faint, but I kept on receiving the impressions."

Yvonne was aware that this consciousness trapped in the elephant was trying to convey to her that as a punishment he was a prisoner in that, to him, horrible mass of flesh. He retained his own human intelligence and awareness, yet he had only the physical capacity of the elephant.

"I don't know how long I stood there," *she continued*, "but gradually the pins-and-needles sensation flooded me as if the blood in my body had again started circulating. Soon I was my normal self, al-

though a bit shaky. I found my husband and was thankful he did not laugh at what I told him.

"Many times after that I returned to the zoo hoping for some other message, but none came. As I stood and watched Elsie pulling here and there at a few twigs and weeds, swinging her little tail behind . . . I wondered . . . and how I wondered."

Descriptions of spirit planes that have been received through mediums or observed by those mortals who are able to make astral projections to the Etheric plane have pictured it as abounding with beautiful flora and fauna. This is true. Not only are the spirits of all living things still existing, but also those advanced entities who wish to practice horticulture have visualized masses of new vegetation. Many creative spirits have thus devised new species, covering much of our plane with beauties such as you have never imagined. Even though all these have been created by thought, they are as real as everything else here is real. Low and unenlightened spirits whose minds cling closely to their former habits and habitats are not able to see the splendor here because they are concentrating only on sordid, dark, and unpleasant conditions. But the rest of us live in what I have already said is truly paradise.

Those of you who love particular pets will be glad to know that they can remain with you if you wish. When you pass into the spirit world your cat, dog, horse, monkey, bird, or any other pet upon which you have lavished affection, is with you when it dies if you want it to be. It is your love of them that enables them to continue to remain with you. If you desire it, they may even accompany you as you progress to higher planes . . . and some dogs and cats, particularly, have accompanied their spirit friends to very high advancement.

The strange powers of the beasts—which you on earth cannot explain—are psychic powers. Telepathy is so strong in all animals that it accounts for much of their behavior that you have not been able to comprehend.

Many dogs know when their masters are coming home long before any person in the house has heard his footsteps or his automobile or his bicycle or his motorcycle. It is not, as zoologists claim, because the dog's hearing is so unnaturally sharp. It is because the dog knows telepathically when his master turns his thoughts toward home, and therefore can anticipate his arrival. If you suddenly decide to take your dog for a walk and he runs for his leash even before you have made a move toward getting up, he has read your thoughts. Your cat may sit and stare at you and then make the appropriate dash for the kitchen when you have decided to feed it, even though it may not be the cat's usual feeding time. Mind to mind, animals are in contact with their own species also to the extent that they have no need for a language. It has often puzzled people to see that their pets seem to understand each other without barking, whining, mewing, or apparently conversing in any way.

It is well known that animals can trail their owners or return to their homes over vast distances. If it were a matter of mere tracking, it could be attributed to the highly competent sense of smell in the animal; but in these days of automation, many pets find their way home after having been carried miles away from it in cars or crated in boxes on planes or trains. It is recorded that certain cats and dogs have even followed their owners to new locations where they have never been before. One cat left behind in Poughkeepsie, New York, when its owner, a veterinarian, moved his family to California, arrived at the West Coast home one year later. How did he do this? He was never out of touch with the humans he loved. Telepathy knows no boundaries of time or space. The animal's mind continued to be in contact with the minds of his owners no matter how far away they went, and he followed them, to their complete amazement.

It should not now be difficult for you to understand homing and migrations. The migratory routes of birds, eels, salmon, turtles, moths, and other creatures that follow the same paths endlessly can be explained as thought patterns read telepathically by them. Early travelers of each species established the routes and returned by their psychical contact with their homes. Their thoughts left what might be described as a path for them to follow the next season, and their issue continued to trace the same paths. All thoughts, as I have said, constitute a physical force. A thought constantly repeated is reinforced to the extent that it becomes so strongly imbedded in reality as to be an actual thing. To the creatures these routes are as plainly marked as roadways or much used footpaths are to you. Keep this in mind the next time you attempt to explain migrations to someone. It makes sense when you think about it.

ANIMALS ARE FOREVER

COMMENTARY:

After receiving such information as this from James and being rather appalled at how unscientific the ideas must appear to others, it delights me to come upon statements of a similar nature in the works of respected scientific writers. In Supernature *British biologist Lyall Watson sees evidence for telepathy between animals— even animals who are distant from each other. He quotes Sir Alister Hardy, once professor of zoology at Oxford:*

"Perhaps our idea on evolution may be altered if something akin to telepathy . . . was found to be a factor in moulding the patterns of behaviour among members of a species. If there was such a non-conscious group behaviour plan, distributed between, and linking, the individuals of the race, . . . it might operate through organic selection to modify the course of evolution."

As an example of this, Watson describes the blue tit, which in Western Europe has recently learned to open the foil caps of milk bottles left on doorsteps and drink the cream off the top. This pattern of behavior among the tits is spreading rapidly throughout Europe, and it might seem to be by imitation, one bird of another. Unless the dairies change the kind of containers they are using, Watson believes that it is possible that these little birds will "develop a bill better designed to exploit a valuable new source of food." He goes on, "Adaptations produced by the animal's own patterns of behaviour are much less predetermined and can lead it out of the niche into the exploration and colonization of entirely new ways of life. Otters would never have developed their webbed feet, nor dolphins their flippers, if one of their entirely terrestrial ancestors had not deviated from its usual routine and gone paddling instead."

And this, he believes, is where telepathy enters the picture. It is true that some of these changes in behavior and body form took place in a relatively short space of time, and it is difficult for Watson to see how the "trial-and-error experiments of occasional adventurous individuals" could have been the only cause. Such things as the milk-drinking tits could certainly spread by imitation, but how does one explain the fact that their new techniques have spread at such a rate that they alarm the dairies? And what about a certain group of monkeys on one of the Japanese islands who have started to take sweet potatoes down to the sea to wash them before eating? Perhaps they are learning new behavior patterns by watching oth-

ers. But how do we account for the fact that monkeys on a neighboring island have also recently begun rinsing their food?

"The existence of an unconscious telepathic link among members of the same species could be a great help in developing and stabilizing new behaviour patterns," says Watson.

Whately Carington, who once experimented with the telepathic transmission of drawings between people and then put forth the idea that other patterns, such as the intricate webs of some spiders, might be communicated in the same way, said in Telepathy: "I suggest that the instinctive behaviour of this high order or elaborate type may be due to the individual creature concerned being linked up into a larger system (or common unconscious if you prefer it) in which all the web-spinning experience of the species is stored up."

Referring to this, Lyall Watson says that it is nonsense to suggest that "instinctive behaviour is governed by a collective unconscious." We know beyond doubt, he says, that it is controlled by genetic inheritance. And yet it is possible that telepathy "could be useful before a habit becomes genetically fixed." He thinks the habit could be spread and stabilized very effectively by some kind of telepathic system. Without it, he finds it difficult to understand how an elaborate instinctive pattern can develop at all in invertebrate animals, which are not likely to acquire new habits by imitation or tradition.

Watson suggests that for a system of this kind to work "news of a new discovery would have to be generally broadcast in the same way as an alarm call. . . ."

XX

SUICIDE IS NOT RECOMMENDED

THERE ARE OCCASIONS when a person suddenly commits a crime, or even takes his own life, with no apparent possible excuse. Even someone who seems to be quite happy and without any depressing problems may commit suicide. The facts, if they were known, would usually reveal that some intruding spirit has caused this unfortunate act. I do not say this to frighten you but to warn you that such things are possibilities.

At the other extreme regarding suicide, a friend of Susy's who had read some of the earlier chapters of this book asked why an individual with a good bit of spiritual development might not decide to take his own life in order to hurry into a future existence where things are bound to be easier because you do not have a body to care for and you do not have the worries of making a living. With the advancement he has now, the questioner presupposed, this individual surely would not be earthbound and would know enough to start his progression right away. So even if suicide caused harder work for a while, would it not be worth it?

While understanding that I have made the higher reaches of the Astral so appealing that one might have a desire to hurry to this afterlife, I must confess that I can only think of this question as indicating an extremely juvenile point of view. I am reminded of a five-year-old boy who decides that adults who are on their own seem to have such an independent existence that he would like to emulate them. And so he packs his little bag and trudges off to the big city to make his fortune. Even if his parents do not come to fetch him and he is allowed to remain there on his own, would he not have an appallingly much more difficult time of it than if he had stayed with his parents until he was grown and then had taken the step forward alone?

You must realize that nobody escapes any of his problems by committing suicide; he quadruples them instead. A man has a responsibility to everyone he loves and even to those he just barely knows if his life somehow might affect them. It is his obligation to himself as well as to them to fulfill every commitment as completely and successfully as possible. If he does not do this on earth, he must conclude it in the spirit world. And if he causes a great deal of trauma to numerous people by his suicide, then he has much more to make up for.

I will devise an illustration in which it will be seen how a man's obligations to others are made much more complicated because of his suicide. Arthur Brown had become involved with Helen MacGregor, who was married and had three children. It seemed impossible that she should ask her husband for a divorce, and yet Helen and Arthur were sure that life would be meaningless without each other. Arthur lived with his mother, and he had always felt himself unable to leave her and make a life of his own because of his compassion for her. Yet he was so oppressed by her constant demands on him that he longed to escape.

As time went on Arthur became more and more melancholy. Suicide is never a thing one deliberately does until a lot of mental pressure has built up, but intense unhappiness and despondency finally caused Arthur to decide to escape—or so he hoped. One day while his mother was out shopping, he tightly closed all the windows and doors of the apartment he shared with her, and turned on the gas. By the time she returned he was dead. Yet Brown's spirit was standing right there in the room when his mother found his body and nearly had a heart attack. Shunning all companionship after his death and in ill health from then on, her first reaction was intolerable grief for some weeks. Then she began to blame him in her thoughts for having perpetrated such a cruel trick on her. She felt that he had deserted her, and she soon worked up almost a loathing for his memory because of what he had done to her. This woman became a recluse, morose and miserable because of her hatred for her son.

If, while he was living, his mother had known of his affair with Helen MacGregor, she would have resented it terribly at first, thinking he had rejected her for another. Yet as time went on she would have become used to the marriage and eventually would have grown fond of Helen. She would even have become a doting grandmother to Helen's children . . . for, yes, if Arthur had held out a while longer he would have been able to marry Helen and make a happy home for her and her family. Her husband, too, was eager to get out of their marriage and it was inevitable that they would have split up over something. So happiness would have been in store for all of them had Arthur not taken the fool's way out.

Now, in his invisible state after his death, Arthur was forced to watch his mother changing from a gracious parent he had loved even when he had resented her to a bitter woman filled with animosity, and he realized it was his fault. As soon as he began to learn the importance of starting his progression, he became aware that her condition was now his responsibility, so he was tied to her even more profoundly than he had ever been on earth. He tried to impress her with the fact that he was still with her, still loved her, but her thoughts toward him were closed and he could never get through to her.

Arthur Brown had other major problems, none of which he had anticipated when he took his life. Helen MacGregor had truly loved him and had been crushed by his death, for she felt responsible for it. Her life now suddenly shattered, she was unable to regain possession of herself, and she started drinking heavily. Her husband and her children were neglected. This eventually gave MacGregor the excuse he had been wanting, and he left her. He would have left for one reason or another anyway, for a separation for this ill-matched couple had been inevitable. Had Arthur still been alive, within two years he and Helen would have married and been very happy. Arthur would have made a fine father for her children, who instead grew up without proper parental discipline. In his invisible state Arthur now realized that he was accountable for all the persons involved with his life who had changed for the worse because he did not remain to face his responsibilities.

This example illustrates that no man escapes his problems by killing himself. He only magnifies them. He has to make amends not only to those whom he would have been able to help while on earth, but he has to assist many others to make up for all those he had not yet met who might have been influenced for the better had he continued to live. Brown's existence after death was vastly more complicated in every way because he took what he thought was the easy way out instead of remaining until his proper time to die and coming over in the state of development he could have attained.

Make no mistake, nothing good can ever come of suicide, and a terrible amount of unhappiness, misery, and misfortune is always caused by it. No matter how miserable he may become, no one in his right senses should ever allow himself to take this way out of his difficulties. And certainly do not ever consider it because you think you have achieved enough advancement on earth and are ready for the joys of future existence. That would be the most fantastic misconception of all.

There is enough to occupy one in the earlier stages of Etheric existence without adding to the load. And, believe me, suicide would add so much weight to your shoulders and cause you so much additional effort in order to make up for the experiences of your earth life that you cut short by your precipitate act that there is no acceptable excuse for it under any circumstances. And the extra problems that you place on others by your suicide are your responsibility. You have to find ways to make amends for them, even though it might take you hundreds of years.

COMMENTARY:

If it will be of any value here, I don't mind admitting that there were two times in my life when I wanted to kill myself to get out from under my seemingly unendurable anguish. Both were primarily over love affairs, because I'm like that, with the addition also of illness and pain and other unhappy situations that made my life unbearable.

The first time I felt that way I actually tried to take my life. It was raining, on top of everything else, and that depressed me even more, so I went to my doctor, ostensibly for the pain of my arthritis, but actually for some sleeping pills. Sensing my misery, he very wisely prescribed a liquid instead of tablets. That night I wrote my farewell note and started to terminate myself abruptly, but I gagged on the medicine before I could get down too much of it. What I took knocked me out, and I awoke the next morning to singing birds and sunshine. It was easy then to be glad that my attempt had been foiled.

This experience occurred before I knew anything about the possibility of a continuance of life after death, at a time when I was agnostic. Had I been told then that I would have to make up afterward for all I didn't accomplish in my life, I would have sneered. Now, the idea presented here by James gives me goose bumps to think of all the extra work I'd have had to do had my attempt succeeded.

There is a humorous saying by those who believe in strict observance of the Sabbath that in heaven you will have to rip out with your nose all the stitches you have ever sewed on a Sunday. Well, by Jove, I believe it would be no less difficult trying to write all the books I have since written . . . if I had nothing to use but a typewriter manufactured by my thoughts. I'm a lousy visualizer. And then somehow getting my messages through to all those people who have since written me about how much assistance my books have given them! What an impossible task!

My second period of great unhappiness, when I contemplated suicide again, occurred in the summer of 1963, when I was once again unsuccessfully convalescing from what I thought was a broken romance. (In this case it turned out to be only a misapprehension on my part.) I went on a European tour and managed, to boot, to fracture my foot in Italy. After several further misadventures I found myself in the Ospedale Internazionale in Naples with my foot in a cast, in a room with a terrace overlooking the beautiful bay. For a month I sat out there on the terrazza alone every evening, the suffering for my lost love even worse because of the magnificent sunsets, the shimmering moonlight. Additionally irritating was the fact that among so many foreigners I had not a soul with whom I could communicate in English or share either my unhappiness or the beauty surrounding me.

My thoughts were constantly on the miserable uselessness of my life; but by then, fortunately, I had been interested in ESP and survival research for several years. I had attempted to communicate with my mother, and James had been giving me messages on the typewriter. I still wasn't thoroughly convinced that I was really talking with spirits of the dead, but I was taking the idea under consideration. And I had received enough information about what a no-no suicide is that I knew better than to try it. I strongly suspected by then that no matter how badly life treats you, that phase will eventually be over and you will go on to better times. So the only thing for me to do, it seemed, was to delight in my lovely lonely vista and shut up about it—building character like mad, no doubt, but, as far as I could see, doing nothing else of any value for myself or humanity.

When I eventually returned to my New York City home, foot somewhat healed and heart stitched together with basting thread, I sat down at my typewriter and complained to James. I really expected him to feel sorrier for me than he did, but he seemed to take my ordeals quite in stride. He wrote:

"It is not really important in the overall result of man's life on earth whether or not he is especially happy all the time, or even much of the time. Although a cheerful existence is devoutly to be desired, and with proper effort on his part at positive thinking one should certainly be able to achieve it, happiness is not the goal of living. Become complete and successful as an individual and then contentment will be revealed in your life as a result of your inner serenity. If it is not possible for you to live in jubilance during your time on earth, it will come later, so do not worry about it.

"There is such great rapture in future planes of life that the small amount that can be enjoyed on earth is inconsequential . . . even though you do not believe me when I say so. To live in a state of eternal overwhelming ecstasy is your destiny, and if you do not have it today, you will not remember tomorrow that it was lacking. You already know that this is true. If you have been very sad for a period of time and then something wonderful like a new sweetheart comes to you so that you are glowingly happy, you spend no time recalling the past months during which you were sad. Because I know it is your ultimate destiny to be at all times joyously alive, vibrant, peaceful, and blessed, I cannot weep for you now if you feel that you have missed out on a few privileges and sensations during your earth life. Earth is your spawning place. For you to worry about not achieving happiness now is as if a young salmon were crying because he had no room to swim in the little stream where he was born, not aware that he would soon be cavorting in the magnificent ocean with all *the space in the world at his disposal and scant memory of his early beginnings."*

No matter how enthralling this news is, I must state that when you're as completely miserable as I had been in Italy you just don't care about what is going to happen to you in the hereafter. It's right now when you need the assistance. That's the time when you should know about calling angels, but I wasn't aware of them then. Had hundreds of James' paragraphs on eternal ecstasy been available, they really might not have helped much. When you're as down as all that, the promise of a lot of lemon pie in the sky and beatific bliss while floating around up yonder sometime in the future doesn't bring much consolation.

And yet I know now that not one of you who reads this book will ever, no matter what the terrible provocation, be likely to take your own life. You may not believe a word you've been reading here. Nonetheless there will always be that tiny doubt: What if James is right? What if he could possibly know whereof he speaks? You'd be a fool to take the chance he might be wrong.

XXI

OUT-OF-THE-BODY TRAVEL

THE EXPERIENCE known as out-of-the-body travel, or astral projection, has been mentioned several times in this book. This is the closest thing to the death experience that can occur while a mortal is alive and physically sound. For this reason it deserves your close attention. It may be one of the ways for you eventually to prove life after death.

What happens in an astral projection is that the soul or spirit or consciousness of an individual leaves its body while it is in a sleeping or comatose or sometimes just resting state and travels about, frequently into the spirit world. It has become increasingly important to researchers to obtain evidence of such experiences so that science can verify their actuality, and such evidence has been acquired on numerous occasions. There is enough genuine documentation that there should be no question in your mind about the actual occurrence of out-of-the-body travel. Millions of people have experienced it.

Out-of-body experiences come about most frequently at night, when they are usually taken for dreams. These are seldom remembered, and never verifiable scientifically, yet they provide one of the most successful forms of spirit communication. When one is ostensibly dreaming of a visit with deceased loved ones, he is frequently actually having a chat with them in the Astral plane.

While it is possible consciously to project out of the body in some cases, the experiences usually occur spontaneously at first and are frequently quite surprising. An individual may be lying on his bed and suddenly find his consciousness at the ceiling looking down at his body below. If he relaxes and does not become frightened, he may then leave his room and travel about, having all kinds of interesting experiences before he finally returns to his body, which, during this time has probably been in a comatose state. The reuniting may be painful or gentle, depending upon the amount of tension or fright involved.

During astral projections, people have found themselves visiting the homes of friends, where they have observed what was going on and have later been able to verify the truth of their perceptions; or they have visited strange places where they had never been before. It is possible for some individuals to have astral projections at will, and they have learned to keep records of their travels and the interesting events they have witnessed.

One form of this phenomenon is known as bilocation, when an astral traveler may be seen in two places at once. His body is observed at home apparently sleeping and his "ghost" or spiritual body or etheric double is seen and recognized somewhere else. The individual may not even be aware of it at the time he is having this experience.

When the consciousness controls its out-of-the-body travels, it is able to bring back definite information, which it had no normal way of knowing. For that reason, this particular type of experience is referred to as traveling clairvoyance. It is possible to test some who have this ability, and psychical researchers have occasionally done so.

COMMENTARY:
The most interesting work of this nature being done today is by the American Society for Psychical Research under the leadership of Dr. Karlis Osis, director of research. He has instigated a wide talent search for people who have OOB experiences at will and can exercise their perception at points far from the physical body. So far the star of Dr. Osis' experimentation has been Ingo Swann, who, as I mentioned earlier, is able to move or alter objects by the power of his mind. He can also often astrally travel to test locations and bring back the specific data requested.

Those who are able to visit spirit dimensions when they are out of their bodies and conscious at the time return with remarkable accounts of their surveillance of conditions in the Astral plane, much of which tallies with what I have related in this book. The brilliant Swedish scientist Emanuel Swedenborg spent the last twenty-seven years of his life making daily visits into every possible area of our world that is attainable by a mortal. He clearly understood what he was seeing, talked to wise and enlightened spirits, and reported his observations intelligently. (Swedenborg, incidentally, has been with me from time to time as I have written this book, and his inspiration has given strength to all who have been involved.)

Because such persons as Swedenborg, no matter how high their status in society, have been unable to prove that they have actually crossed the border between planes of existence, their accounts are usually attributed to imagination, religious zeal or mysticism. Fortunately Swedenborg had previously provided such genuine evidence of clairvoyance—and he was such a superior citizen—that his evidence has been looked on with more favor than that of most others who have had adventures of a similar nature.

But what exactly is an out-of-the-body experience? Let me explain with an analogy: Since the consciousness resides in and about the physical body just as if it were his home, an astral projection occurs when this "occupant" leaves for a brief visit somewhere else. The subconsciousness, who is the caretaker or janitor, does not dare to leave, however, or the body-house will die.

When one's consciousness is away from home, the house could be considered vacant. An earthbound entity who discovers this might easily be tempted to move in, and then the returning owner would find his body possessed. For this reason, unless the astral projection is spontaneous, or unless you have had them so frequently that you know just how to handle yourself, it is not wise to force such experiences and take the chance of intruders.

If an astral projection occurs to you spontaneously, however, relax and enjoy it as an interesting new escapade. There is little chance of danger because such a projection would not be spontaneous unless the situation were just right for it.

It is interesting that when bilocation occurs, the subject of ghosts may come up. It might on occasion be possible for someone to see an astral traveler whom he had known to be alive only a short time previously. He would most likely have a great fright thinking his friend had died suddenly. If this out-of-the-body traveler happens to be observed by a stranger, he may be taken for a ghost who is haunting the place where he is seen. Certainly it would be difficult to convince the startled observer that he has been confronted by the ghost of a living human being. But that is exactly what has happened.

Out-of-the-body experiences present your researchers with evidence that there is something within the physical body that can leave it and function intelligently outside the organism. And, if you but realize it, such experiences are the best possible evidence that there is something that can leave the body and continue to function intelligently after death.

COMMENTARY:

I have quoted evidential cases of this sort in many of my books and do not intend to repeat them here, but there is one woman who had some experiences that so delightfully confirm much of what James has said that I must share her story with the reader. She was Harriet M. Shelton, a dear little lady who died several years ago at an advanced age. I knew her when I lived in New York City, when she gave me some of her accounts of out-of-the-body experiences for my book The Enigma of Out-of-Body Travel. *They were confirmed as nearly as possible by the Reverend Gladys Custance of Onset, Massachusetts, with whom Miss Shelton had studied clairvoyance.*

On nights when Gladys and her husband, Reverend Kenneth Custance, held meetings in Onset, Miss Shelton, who was in her New York apartment, would sometimes attempt to visit them by astral projection. No one at the Onset meeting knew she had any such intention the first time she attempted such projection on a Friday in March, 1963. But suddenly during the evening two young women spoke up at the same time, saying, "There's Miss Shelton." They had actually seen her phantom. For the sake of evidence I have checked with them both and verified Miss Shelton's story. They really did see her; no one had been talking about her, and there was no possible reason that they should have thought of her at that moment—unless what they declared to be true was.

Now, with this corroborative testimony that she does have legiti-

mate astral projections, here are her unverifiable accounts of her visits to the spirit world: "On the planes I have visited," she said, "the dirt roads wind along, up and down through wooded areas where the trees meet overhead. There are roadside flowers which are more vivid in color than ours, and I am told that they never fade. Birds flit from tree to tree, and an occasional rabbit crosses the road ahead. Now and then a house by the roadside seems to be a replica of some much-loved home on earth. My father's Astral country place is almost an exact copy of one he had in Ridgefield." There Miss Shelton visited often with her parents and her deceased husband.

Among the most charming of her tales are her observances of children, whom she found enjoying themselves in grassy bowers and running and splashing in the water, with no one to tell them, "Don't do this, it's dangerous," or "Stop that, you'll get hurt."

The more adventurous children were diving in and out of a lake and playing under a waterfall. Then, as she stood watching them, she saw a number of boys running along the shore in great excitement and she realized they were having a race. "You will never believe me when I tell you," she said, "that porpoises were leaping along through the water with small boys clinging to their backs. Then, out of the woods, to my astonishment, hopped two enormous bright green frogs with boys riding them!"

The most enchanting of Miss Shelton's stories occurred when she was spending the summer in an apartment in Onset. She was sitting one afternoon with Gladys Custance when she went into trance and was taken by her spirit guide whom she called "the professor" for a visit to the Animal Kingdom. There, after various encounters with wildlife, she met a handsome black-maned lion. As he walked slowly toward her she asked her guide if it would be safe to touch him.

"Speak to him first, and see how he responds," was the answer. But this was unnecessary, for the lion came up to her and rubbed his head against her knees. Just then on the earth plane Gladys Custance's large black dog, Rastus, burst through the door of the room in which the two ladies were sitting, and flopped down on the floor in front of his mistress' feet.

"The lion looked up and saw Rastus and walked over to him," said Miss Shelton. And Rastus saw the lion! He let out a wild yelp and tore out of the room and down the stairs as fast as he could go. And he would never come up into her apartment again.

"Many people have asked me how Rastus, who was in Onset, and the lion, who was in the Celestial Animal Kingdom, could see each other," said the astral traveler. "I asked the professor about this. He explained that animals are more psychic than people and can tune in to certain vibrations which are present, under just the right conditions."

"Whatever these conditions are," I concluded my account in Enigma, "they should be encouraged by all concerned. Life couldn't help but be sweeter in a land where a lion acts just like a big old pussy cat."

XXII

QUESTIONS AND ANSWERS

I WILL NOW attempt to answer some of the questions posed by those who have read this material during the time it has been in manuscript form.

QUESTION: It is difficult to believe that some persons who have been responsible for genocide and mass persecutions can ever achieve Ultimate Perfection. Are you sure there is not a traditional flaming hell for these?

ANSWER: There is definitely a hell for such human beasts, and they exist in it for a long, long time before they have finally made amends, as much as it is ever possible to make amends, for the terrible grief they have caused. This is not a hell of fire and brimstone, but of hatred and bitterness among others as loathsome as they. Existence seems entirely without hope for them until they begin to realize the depths of their degradation; but when they finally face up to the extent of their crimes, their hell is even worse, for they are so appalled by the horror of their deeds. Eventually they will work out of it, for so great is the love of Divine Consciousness for all humanity that all are included in it, no matter how low they might once have been. Even these regenerated mass murderers will one day receive the forgiveness of other advanced spirits and come to be able to forgive themselves, and then they will start their advancement.

It is also true—and you must face it even though you don't want to—that most of such brutes are actually insane. Their minds have been unable to function properly during the time they were in positions of power and they were not capable of thinking intelligently about what they were doing or ordering others to do. Those who because of their greed and avarice have allowed insane persons to hold positions of power and have followed their orders are as much at fault as they and will have even more remorse when their progression starts and they realize what they have done. The insane are cared for here in hospitals or nursing homes until they finally return to normal. Some take longer than others; but all will eventually regain their proper manner of thinking and begin to advance as everyone else does.

Imagine the great love of humanity demanded of the workers who staff these hospitals, when they realize that they are having to assist in the regeneration of a Hitler or a Stalin and must always provide them with compassionate care.

QUESTION: If God is all-encompassing perfection, how can he allow such imperfection to exist?

ANSWER: There is an explanation for this: If all were perfect, there would be no way for improvement, and God—Divine Consciousness—is always improving and expanding. Negatives exist so that positives can be recognized. It would not be possible thoroughly to understand Good if we did not have Evil as a contrast.

When Supreme Intelligence decided to personify certain aspects of itself, it chose to use the form of man for this purpose. As man lives he undergoes emotions of all kinds so that he can comprehend all varieties of experience. He must come to understand goodness and love; but he must also have the contrast of evil and unwholesomeness, for how can he truly know perfection unless he has known imperfection? If one were born perfect and had no life on earth where evil exists, would he be able fully to appreciate Ultimate Perfection when he achieved it?

COMMENTARY:

Or, as Pope John XXIII said, "*If God created shadows it was in order to better emphasize the light.*"

In the manuscript The Upward Path, James told Miss Underhill: "Many of you may say: 'I don't see why God didn't make us perfect in the beginning.' Why make a static universe or a being without dynamic force, without the desire or capacity to evolve?

"You should be elated to think that the Plan of World-Growth is to be furthered through your individual efforts. Can you not see the great wisdom, the infinitely greater Purpose, of God's Evolutionary Soul-Plan, which allows each individual to find Reality and make Reality his own?"

QUESTION: A reader wonders how advanced spirits can achieve perfection and still retain a conscious awareness of self. This seems to her to contrast with the idea of nirvana and the samadhi state of the occult religions, in which the entire intent is to achieve a condition of selflessness or egolessness. In metaphysical circles such words as "consciousness" and "state of awareness" and "self" and "personality" have acquired a certain negative stigma. Certainly no one who is spiritually enlightened, this woman implied, as tactfully as possible, should be so narcissistic as to wish to survive eternally as *himself*. She suggests that unless he attains a state of complete selflessness he has not developed sufficiently. Wanting to retain personal identity after death somehow becomes a most egotistical desire, which should be suppressed at all costs.

The woman who presented this problem to James has been a student of metaphysics for years, and she has had some beautiful experiences. Through using certain yoga techniques she has once or twice undergone illumination, and she maintains that the great sublimity of it was the fact that she had lost herself in it completely. She was sure that nirvana, the ultimate achievement for the yogi, would be just like this, a complete losing of one's identity. "When you think about who it is happening to," she said, "the experience leaves you."

ANSWER: Life after death is in no way like what this woman thinks it will be. Besides being a state of all-encompassing Love and Bliss, God is also Intellect and Mind and Wisdom. When you attain complete awareness of your unity with God, it is a knowledge that your mind is one with the Universal Mind. Divine Consciousness is *conscious*, not unconscious. And so are you, always. Even while you are on earth there is no moment in your conscious life when awareness is not present, for without it you would be asleep, in a trance, anesthetized or in a coma. When you are having your deepest periods of illumination—at times when *what* you are seeing or experiencing is altogether more important than *who* is experiencing it—there is still the experiencer in the background.

As part of your development after death you will learn to be able to retain an alert awareness of self at the same time that you are having these great illuminating experiences of oneness and unity with God. And when you enjoy the rapture of Illimitable Love, you will know who is experiencing it and be able to hold on to that knowledge, not lose it.

Time will go on, you know, and so will the young lady who asked the question. If she thinks one who has achieved the heights is eternally basking in bliss and doing nothing else, she will be greatly surprised when she begins her progression after death and learns of all the work there is to do. As an active component of Supreme Intelligence, she must be about her Father's business.

Certainly, I say to her, you will maintain this shining light of elation. But it is *you* who has it, not some amorphous entity who is all radiance and no individuality. You would be more likely to thank God for occasional brief interludes of samadhi than an eternity of it. The wonderful thing about achieving Ultimate Perfection is that you have that same rapture at all times, while still being aware of yourself as an individual and consciously attending to your duties . . . as well as your pleasures. You will be an exalted soul who once was a specific human being and who has not forgotten it.

COMMENTARY:

Perhaps what James is expressing is described by Martin Israel in an essay titled "The Nearness of God" in Life, Death and Psychical Research. *The essay describes an experience he had when he was a sixteen-year-old boy. He writes: "The organ of perception cannot be defined in earthly language. I 'saw' but not with my earthly eye; I 'heard' but not with my worldly ears. The nearest scientific description would be that I 'sensed' with an inner, hidden organ of perception that included all five senses in a magnified, expanded awareness, and that this could be correlated by an inner organ of intelligence which could comprehend divine purpose and function in the information vouchsafed. I was above creation, and the organ of perception and intelligence could divine the onward flow of life in the cosmos. . . . Though I never ceased to be my true self, I was no longer a separate, circumscribed person, but was one with all creation in my unique identity, which merged with, and added its essence to, the created whole. It was an expanded consciousness that I had ceased to be aware of as my own separation. . . ."*

I know it is incomprehensible now to the woman who asked the question that she will ever want anything more exciting than the illumination she has had; but there is sublimity completely undreamed of in the wildest imaginings of anyone on earth. I, at my level of achievement high in the Astral, have only heard of how wondrous it will someday be. What I have experienced here is illumination completely beyond anything possible on earth; but it is still far from what will eventually be my constant state . . . and your constant state.

QUESTION: Through hypnosis many people are today being age regressed to past lives. How do you explain this if reincarnation is not true?

ANSWER: Because it is possible for a few individuals to live a second life, as I have explained, by possessing the body of a baby and remaining in it throughout its lifetime, it can happen that an occasional age regression might tap memories of the previous existence. This is rare, but it does occur. However, if more than one past life is brought out at this time, you can be sure that there are other explanations, for no entity who has ever had to assimilate the memories of two lifetimes will ever be so careless as to attempt another birth.

Genetic memory may produce information about the life of an ancestor when one is attempting unconsciously to provide data for the hypnotist. A third, and probably more likely explanation is that when an individual is hypnotized, he may go into a mediumistic trance. Then a spirit can speak through him just as it would through an entranced medium.

COMMENTARY:

Someone has pointed out that if a hypnotist tells you that you are a monkey and you begin to act like one, it does not mean that you were a monkey in a former incarnation. But if he tells you you are age regressed and asks you to produce a past life for him, he tends to believe that whatever you tell him is factual. And when you hear about it later after you are out of hypnosis, you believe it, too.

Many people think that the famous Bridey Murphy was, instead of a former incarnation of Ruth Tighe, actually a possessing spirit who moved into her body and talked while she was hypnotized into a mediumistic trance.

In hypnosis, the subject, having placed himself under the influence of the hypnotist's mind, will endeavor to give him whatever he asks for. Thus, the most normal and usual explanation for what seems to be past-life recall is that when the hypnotist tells you he has regressed you past birth and asks for memories of a former life, you readily supply him with something that answers that requirement. You do not rationalize in the hypnotic trance state whether or not you are telling the truth, you only afford him what he wants, for you have made your will subservient to his.

COMMENTARY:

An interesting study of hypnotic age regression supposedly to a past life was done by Edwin S. Zolik of Marquette University and published in the Journal of Clinical Psychology, 1958. *A male volunteer was hypnotized and then told that he was being age regressed to a previous existence. He then claimed to be Brian O'Malley of County Cork, an officer in Her Majesty's Irish Guard, who had been born in 1850. He told of his many flirtations with pretty French and Irish girls. He'd had a mistress, he said, but no wife; and he had been killed in 1892 at the age of forty-two when he fell from his horse while jumping hurdles.*

Four days later the subject was again deeply hypnotized and not age regressed. He was then asked for the truth about Brian O'Malley. He recalled that a Timothy O'Malley (not Brian), whose description answered all the details he had given as a past life, was actually a man his grandfather had known and had later come to despise. Since the youth also felt that his grandfather had hated him and that the hatred had involved his riding a mare when he had been told not to, there seemed to be an identification in his mind with the O'Malley man. Zolik states by way of summary:

"*Analysis of the two hypnotic sessions indicated that the principal character of the 'previous existence' fantasy, Brian O'Malley, had a significant emotional relationship with the subject's grandfather, who, in turn played a major role in the subject's childhood and early adolescence. Due to a severe emotional incident in childhood, the subject perceived himself as being rejected by his grandfather, and to minimize this threat patterned, in fantasy, his aspirations to accord with his grandfather's desires. The career to which the subject aspired as a child was similar in nature to that of this close friend of his grandfather, and the major components of this 'previous existence' were based on stories which his grandfather had told about this friend." The fantasy appeared to be dynamically related in this case to a major emotional conflict that was repressed.*

This, of course, is just one incident, but it could indicate the possibility that some other events described as past-life recall might have a similar psychogenic basis.

When you are in a deep state of hypnotic trance, your consciousness may abdicate your body entirely, just as an entranced medium's does. But a medium has sat for development of his abilities before he starts going into trance and has guides and other spirit associates who have worked with him and know how to protect him, while a hypnotist's subject is unlikely to have this kind of protection. Therefore, it is possible on occasion for a spirit entity to take over a hypnotized person's body. This is why it is sometimes difficult to bring someone out of hypnosis. The intruder may not want to leave. For this reason more than any other, hypnosis should never be played with by amateurs, and all doctors who use it should be aware of the possibility of possession. Since medics are slow to accept anything but a materialistic concept, they may recognize danger in hypnosis when used by others, but it is hardly likely they will recognize the true danger and admit the possibility of spirit influence being involved.

QUESTION: It is not easy to convince most people that they are godlike creatures, because life in most cases is so mundane, mercenary and uninspiring. What can we do when the world fences us in like that?

Answer: Go outdoors. As a rule only when one is out in a great pine forest or sitting on top of a hill overlooking the ocean or watching a magnificent desert sunset is it brought home to him what a real part of it all he is. As much as anything, man is of value in the world because of his ability to appreciate. God's need for man is as essential as man's need for God.

God is an Aware Intelligence whose components are all individual people who live and think as individuals, from the time of their origin until and including their return to the Godhead of All-knowingness. It is as if every cell in your body had a separate identity and consciousness, yet all are working together for the common good of the body. Malignant cells that wildly reproduce their own kind without thought for the good of others are the (earthbound) villains. White leukocytes are the hosts of angels who rush around trying to give aid when problems arise. Each cell is an individual and yet all live together as a composite whole. At death the spirits of the cells—the spiritual body—continue to live, while the physical cells die away. This is an old, old concept, yet quite an accurate one. Each human body is a small universe in itself.

For a successful life it is necessary for the cells of the body to work in harmony at all times with the organized unit they are part of. When this does not occur, the body is ill. Most cells have no cognizance of their overall cooperative function or their ultimate destiny. They merely go along as separate individuals just as you do in your lifetimes, completely unaware of the cooperation necessary in order to achieve success for all.

It is at the times one senses his unity with Divine Consciousness that he is most joyous. Those who meditate and are in daily mental touch with their source are among the happiest people. Life should always be for you as inspiring as it is on those rare occasions when you sit on top of a hill and watch the ocean waves roll in or look at a magnificent sunset and feel yourself to be a true functioning unit in the overall majesty of the universe. To be able to keep that realization in your daily life is your goal. It is seldom achieved on earth. In the upper reaches of the first planes after death the necessity to attempt constantly to retain this feeling of oneness with Supreme Intelligence is learned. When one has advanced to the point of angelhood and godhood, he is always aware of it, and he is always jubilant.

When you realize these facts and know for sure that this is your ultimate destiny, you can endure the humdrum problems of life on earth more easily and with less depression. Be one of those who knows! Keep the awareness of your immortality always with you!

QUESTION: It is easy for you disembodied spirits to talk about loving all the time, but for those of us who have to put up with the disagreeable human entities we are always rubbing shoulders with, it is definitely not simple to do. Do you have any secrets as to how to go about it?

ANSWER: It is no easier for us to learn to love than for you. After all, those human entities you refer to turn into spirit entities who are still just as disagreeable. It is actually easier for you to learn it on earth if you start young enough. After you have established bad habit patterns over the years, you have to undo them over here if you haven't done it before. It is better not to establish them in the first place. And so face up to the fact that you need as soon as possible to learn to love everyone, not only those to whom you are attached and who are kind to you. It takes real work to love everyone, but it is the most important single lesson you have to learn; you must set your mind to it and make a start. If you do, everything will go smoothly in your life and you will be happy. Love everyone every minute and your life will be a big success while you are on earth as well as afterward.

Now, after having given you this invigorating encouragement, let me see if I can provide a few pointers for achieving love. In the first place—and you will be delighted to hear this—compassion, understanding and sympathy are reasonable facsimiles and if you can acquire them, then love is not far behind. Make an effort to counteract with something kind all unloving thoughts you have about anyone. Try to be alert to your thoughts, as you no doubt are by now if you are attempting to apply positive thinking as I have taught you. Whenever you find yourself with a negative thought, you are replacing it with a positive one, are you not? All right, whenever you find yourself with any thought about anyone that indicates a lack of appreciation for them, substitute one that is the reverse. If you were to see an ugly person and find the thought in your mind, "Oh, how grotesque he is," replace it with, "but I am sure he must have a beautiful soul." If someone is cross with you and you are tempted to think, "She's a nasty slut," instead force yourself to think, "Oh, no she isn't. She's really good. This is just a bad day for her."

Susy likes the story about the old woman who could think of nothing really constructive to say about a bad boy and would not allow herself to be unkind, so, when everyone else was running him down, she said, "Well, he kin whistle good." Bear this in mind and you will find yourself smiling about someone you nearly hate as you instead think, "Well, he kin whistle good." The very fact that you are able to make a joke about your dislike is a definite step forward.

You can almost make a game of it—trying to think of something nice about people who are unpleasant to you. This really takes effort on your part, most particularly if you live around hateful people; but as you work at it, you are learning compassion for them. One day you will suddenly realize that you do not resent the individual half as much as you previously did, and you will discover that you can now actually force yourself to think of him as a son of God—certainly a misguided one who has a lot to learn but nonetheless one you can accept as a brother. It will surprise you, no doubt, but he will probably not be displaying anywhere near as much animosity toward you as previously. For when you send out thoughts of love, you find them returned.

I do not suggest that this is an easy procedure. It is good hard work. And it takes time, lots of time. But it is definitely worth it in every way, not the least of which will be your own improved self-esteem when you realize what you have accomplished.

QUESTION: I am aware that what you present in this book is philosophy and does not purport to provide evidence; but why can't we in some way get supporting documentation for the situations you describe? When are we going to be able to prove scientifically that what you say is true? So far there seems to be no repeatable test of any kind that can confirm life after death. Do you suppose the day will ever come when there can actually be proof? Or is trying to find it a lost cause?

ANSWER: I am sure that acceptable evidence for life after death will not be long in coming. There are a number of organized activities today reaching in that general direction, and more will follow as time goes on. You will soon find that the words "survival" and "soul" will no longer be naughty words that cannot be mentioned in polite intellectual society. More and more people are coming to admit freely their interest in the possibility of life after death. I hope this book will open more minds and more doors for further research.

As to specific lines of inquiry when the time comes that money for research is available, there are several areas to which I would suggest your efforts be directed. They all depend first on sponsoring and subsidizing certain psychically gifted persons so that they can afford to spend a large amount of their time developing an ability for physical mediumship. It is often asked why "physical" mediumship is of value as a means of proving survival. Psychical energy, or psychokinetic force, is produced in the bodies and from the minds of some humans more than others. When we spirits find persons with these innate capabilities, we attempt to encourage them to build this power as much as possible. It is then available for us to use in our manifestations. It is true that our helping a physical medium to bend teaspoons does not prove survival. However, if this ability were used in other directions, it could supply proof. Here are the lines along which initial research should be instigated:

1. Attempts to receive fingerprints of deceased persons whose prints are already on record have been undertaken before by mediums with highly questionable results. But if you have a strong enough medium and carefully controlled conditions, there is no reason that fingerprints could not be obtained.

2. There are numerous attempts going on today throughout the world to receive voices of spirits on tape recorders. The conditions are in no way perfected, and projection from our end as well as reception from yours is extremely difficult and uncontrollable at the present time. But with a scientific approach to the problems entailed, the time will come when good reception is possible. The goal, of course, is to perfect the techniques so that voices of spirits can be received in sufficient strength and volume to be compared with the voice prints left by these deceased entities before their demise. Much work will have to be done before such efforts will be successful, but that time will definitely come.

3. Spirit photography has occurred frequently but has almost always been questioned as fraud. When enough strong physical mediums are working on this with Polaroid cameras under controlled conditions, results will be spectacular.

When effort in any of these three areas is implemented, it will be possible to obtain proof of life after death. Do not be discouraged if it does not come quickly; with sufficient exertion it *will* come. And do not withhold your efforts in these directions, waiting for the availability of a good medium. Perhaps you researchers yourselves, or some of your friends, may have latent talent in this direction.

COMMENTARY:

A tax-free foundation, which is dedicated entirely to research of this nature – and most especially in the directions indicated by James – is the Survival Research Foundation, of which I have the honor to be the founder and first president. Some of its aims and purposes are to conduct, subsidize, and assist in the procuring of scientific evidence for conscious survival of the human soul or spirit after death, and to establish the results of the research as worthy of public consideration. The current president is Arthur Berger, P.O. box 63-0026, Miami, FL 33163-0026. There is also a Susy Smith Project in the Psychology Department of the University of Arizona, for the purpose of registering your afterlife codes. The Web site for registering is: http://www.afterlifecodes.com/

XXIII

THE END IS JUST THE BEGINNING

As I come to the close of this book, there is really no reason for me to dwell at length about why we in the spirit world are so eager for you on earth to know the truth. It should be self-evident by now that we who are working toward our progression love all of you and want you to put this knowledge to use so that your transitions will be easier than ours were. And think of how much work you will save us if we do not have so many unenlightened newcomers to convert!

Many people do not ever think about the possibility of life after death. But most persons who think, think at one time or another about the subject—usually without achieving any answers that satisfy them. That is why they so often put the question aside, in order not to be embarrassed or confused by it. There are even some who insist that they would not want to survive death consciously. They protest that they do not like themselves enough to feel worthy of survival.

The truth is that your life has been for nothing unless you survive. Why should you go through all the difficulties and torments that each person has to endure if there were no reason for it and no result from it other than the perpetuation of the race? Why should the species man be continued at all, if he came from nowhere by chance coincidence and goes nowhere?

To be extinguished like a light would mean that you remembered no more and suffered no more, it is true. But it would also mean that you nevermore knew joy and love.

For all those who have accepted a completely negative attitude, there are others who have little else except blind faith to give them the assurance they need that they will survive death . . . and to them it is enough. Jesus came back from the dead to prove that he had continued to live and that all men would do likewise. All that I have taught in this book is also in the Bible, although many people interpret the Bible in various ways that might make my statements appear to be at variance with it.

The emphasis, of course, should be placed on the consciousness, the soul, the spirit. That survives death and progresses so successfully that all your worries about the continuance of a personality you may not happen to like should be cast aside. As you advance you become so enlightened that your original nature becomes wondrous and glorious. On earth as you grow more and more involved with helping others, keeping yourself occupied fully with good works, pleasant company, and interesting endeavors you have so little time to think about your own problems that they seldom take precedence. This is the way it is as you grow in spiritual values after death, becoming more and more loving and lovable and less and less self-centered. Do not fret about yourself; you will soon think of your own importance so seldom that it will not matter.

For much too long your psychologists and behaviorists have attempted to convince you that man is a mere machine or even just a beast with a different kind of thinking apparatus. It has been forbidden by your intellectuals to discuss man as a soul or spirit living in a physical body. One has been looked on as naïve if he believed in a life after death, in a soul that could continue to live forever.

It has been evident in recent years that this idea of man as a mechanical unit has given little harmony to the world, no peace and much dissatisfaction to men, for a theory so nihilistic cannot bring happiness. Now you are beginning to realize that in order to survive as successful individuals it is necessary to have a philosophy . . . to know that you are of importance in the scheme of things. There is no way you can achieve true peace of mind until you once again return to the old concept of man as a spirit inhabiting a body. Then you can allow yourself to conjecture about the ultimate destiny of this spirit and its reason for existing. When you finally become aware that the plan of the universe is a perfect plan and that man is a fundamental aspect of it, you will recognize your worth and that of all others.

No one who knows that all men are destined to return to Ultimate Perfection can ever belittle himself or his fellows. No one with such knowledge would be able to use his authority to declare war. He would not kill or in any way deliberately harm another or do anything to hinder the perfect growth of all other human beings and the world in which they live. When you think of yourself as one with Supreme Intelligence, you will act in a responsible manner at all times.

No such concerned man will make his own causes more urgent than those of another, nor his own needs more important. Your ecology problems will resolve themselves when each man thinks more of his neighbor and his neighbor's property than of his own. Your pollution situation will be remedied when care for all the world's beauties and bounties is more important than gain for any individual or group. Overpopulation will recede when everyone learns not to have children until they are able to raise them under nearly ideal conditions. There will be no racial injustices, no inhumanity to man, when all are known to be kindred with the identical beautiful destiny.

Do you want to know how to do yourself a favor? Whenever you have any trouble of any kind, tell yourself who you are. Stop right in the midst of your worrying and say to yourself, "I am a son of God. I am going to live forever. I am so far superior to anything negative that can happen to me that it is inconsequential. I am above worry. My mind dwells on love and happiness, not on sorrow. This situation that is causing me grief will pass away and my life will be better for having endured it without breaking down and letting it conquer me. I will learn from it. I will not let it cause me anguish because a son of God need not suffer."

The Son of God called Jesus the Christ was able to endure a painful death on a cross without breaking down. He was able to say of those who crucified him, "Father, forgive them for they know not what they do." You can say the same. Nothing so horrendous as crucifixion will come to you, but even small cares and troublesome situations can be overcome in the same way, by facing up to them as Jesus would have, not as a sniveling weakling who does not admit to having free will and blames all his inadequacies on his parents and his childhood traumas. Not as a mere mechanical automaton who believes he has no soul will you face your problems, but as one who knows his beautiful destiny. Small aggravations or large woes can not conquer you, for you are immortal!

What could possibly really disturb the equanimity of one at the start of his eternal existence who knows that he is only on the first mile of a journey that will continue forever? It will always be a joyful and exciting life if you think of it that way from now on. It will eventually be that way all the time; why not start on earth to appreciate and enjoy it? I know all of you can do it if you will put your minds to it. I know you have the courage and the endurance and the love to overcome all negatives and sing and shout with joy instead. I want to see you do this with your lives right now.

It is the inevitable destiny of your world to develop to the point that all is serenity. You, by your conscious efforts to love and to think positively will improve yourself and all those who come in contact with you, and you will help the world make its start in the direction of peace and perfection. The fact that this will entail a good bit of work is what will discourage some of you from starting, but the challenge of it will encourage others. I believe that you readers—who by now strongly suspect that what I am telling you is true and that you and all your fellows are eternal—are the ones who are going to take the first giant steps for mankind. And they won't be on some lonely distant moon, but right where you are, inside of each of your lovely souls.

And so it is a large group of us in spirit who send our blessings to you in your endeavors. You will always have our love and our assistance as we all progress together toward our magnificent destiny of Ultimate Perfection.

BIBLIOGRAPHY

BLATTY, WILLIAM PETER, *The Exorcist*. New York, Harper & Row, 1971.
CARINGTON, WHATELY, *Telepathy*. London, Methuen, 1954.
CERMINARA, GINA, *Insights for the Age of Aquarius*. Englewood Cliffs, N.J., Prentice-Hall, 1973.
FODOR, NANDOR, *Between Two Worlds*. West Nyack, N.Y., Parker Publishing Co., 1964.
HARDY, ALISTER, "Biology and ESP," in *Science and ESP*. London, Routledge & Kegan Paul, 1967.
HEYWOOD, ROSALIND, *Journal of the Society for Psychical Research*, Vol. 47, No. 757 (September, 1973).
LODGE, SIR OLIVER, *Raymond*. New York, George H. Doran Co., 1916.
MILLER, DEWITT, *You Take It With You*. New York, The Citadel Press, 1955.
PEARCE-HIGGINS, CANON J. D., ed. with REV. G. STANLEY WHITBY, *Life, Death and Psychical Research*. London, Rider & Co., 1973.
Psychic (April, 1973; Aug., 1973; Feb., 1974).
RAMACHARAKA, YOGI, *The Life Beyond Death*. Yogi Publication Soc., Chicago, Ill., 1912.
Self-Realization (Summer, 1973).
SHERMAN, HAROLD, *Your Mysterious Powers of ESP*. New York, World, 1969.
SMITH, SUSY, *Confessions of a Psychic*, New York, Macmillan, 1971.
——, *The Enigma of Out-of-Body Travel*. New York, Garrett Publications, 1965.
——, *Life Is Forever*. New York, G. P. Putnam's Sons, 1974.
——, *Widespread Psychic Wonders*. New York, Ace, 1970.

Smith, Susy, *World of the Strange*. New York, Pyramid, 1963.
Stevenson, Ian, *Twenty Cases Suggestive of Reincarnation*. American Society for Psychical Research, Vol. 26, 1966.
Teilhard de Chardin, Pierre, *The Phenomenon of Man*. New York, Harper & Row, 1965.
Time (December 24, 1973).
Von Reuter, Florizel, *Psychical Experiences of a Musician*. Waukesha, Wis., Cultural Press, N.D.
Watson, Lyall, *Supernature*. Garden City, N.Y., Anchor Press/Doubleday, 1973.
White, Stewart Edward, *The Unobstructed Universe*. New York, Dutton, 1943.
Wickland, Carl, *Thirty Years Among the Dead*. Los Angeles, National Psychological Institute, 1924.
Zolik, Edwin S., "An Experimental Investigation of the Psychodynamic Implications of the Hypnotic 'Previous Existence' Fantasy." *Journal of Clinical Psychology*, Vol. 14 (1958).

9 781583 485736